London Villages
John Wittich

Shire Publications Ltd

Printed in Great Britain by C. I. Thomas & Sons (Haverfordwest) Ltd, Press Buildings, Merlins Bridge,
Haverfordwest, Dyfed SA61 1XF.

ACKNOWLEDGEMENTS
The publishers are grateful to Peter Matthews for his assistance in the preparation of this book. The
maps of Chelsea, Dulwich, Hammersmith, Islington, Richmond and Stoke Newington are by Richard
G. Holmes. The maps of Clerkenwell and Kensington are by D. R. Darton. The location map on page
4 is by Robert Dizon. Other maps are by Shirley Barker. The photographs on pages 2 and 45 are
reproduced courtesy of Fulham Palace. The other photographs are acknowledged to Cadbury Lamb.

Cover: *Hogarth's House, Chiswick.*

Previous page: *Richmond Bridge.*

Below: *Fulham Palace: the Tudor courtyard.*

Contents

Preface

In the beginning there was the city of London, enclosed by the Romans with a wall in AD 190 and covering 134 hectares. It was surrounded by small villages, where in time people from the city began to settle among the local inhabitants. Commuting has been practised from 'time out of memory' according to John Stow, the famous London historian. Soon the villages were linked to the city by people travelling daily to work.

With the rapid growth of the population, particularly during Tudor times, the city expanded beyond the walls, in spite of several byelaws which were passed to prevent buildings from being erected outside. As early as the twelfth century the city of London was linked to Westminster by the Strand (the roadway by the riverside, as its name implies) and to Southwark (the south ward of the city) by London Bridge. However, it was the growth of the eighteenth and nineteenth centuries that brought about the complete immersion of the outlying villages.

Today London covers over 160,000 hectares, houses between seven and eight million people and stretches from Enfield in the north to Croydon in the south. Yet within this area many of the formerly separate villages continue to exist and retain their own distinctive atmosphere and charm. With a little imagination and with this book to hand it is easy to piece together the remnants of these London villages.

The villages of London that are described in this book.

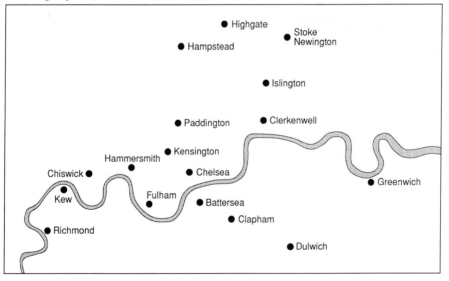

1
Battersea

Mention Battersea to people and they might well react 'Dog's Home', 'Festival Gardens' or even 'Power Station'. Others may well have heard of the Battersea Shield, a fine piece of iron age workmanship now in the British Museum, or of the Battersea (de Morgan) Pottery.

The name is shown as Patricsey Island in the Domesday Survey of 1086 and means Peter's Island, for Battersea was once owned by the monks of Westminster Abbey, whose patron saint was St Peter. After the Reformation and the Dissolution of the Monasteries in the sixteenth century the manor passed to the St John family and the Earls of Spencer, who are still lords of the manor, although there has been no direct connection with the family since the nineteenth century. Before the developments of the late eighteenth and early nineteenth centuries the main occupation of the local inhabitants was market-gardening and one of the main products was simples (medicinal herbs), which were supplied to the apothecaries of London. The saying 'You must go to Battersea to get your simples cut' derives from this side of life in the former village. It is used as a reproof to somebody who has made a foolish observation.

Today Battersea forms part of the borough of Wandsworth, under the London Government Act 1963 and, despite being absorbed into a large municipal authority's area, it still retains much of its village atmosphere.

The origin of the **Battersea Dogs' Home** (1), in Battersea Park Road, was the desire of a Mrs Tealby to do something for the thousands of dogs who ran free in the streets of Victorian London, particularly in the Holloway area of north London. After early problems — neighbours, finance and housing — the home settled in Battersea in 1871. Stray dogs from all over London are brought to the home, and a rate of some sixty a day has been recorded. Since its original opening in north London in 1860 over two million dogs have been taken in and looked after. Conditions of buying a dog from the home — some two thousand are sold every year — are that it will be well cared for and not be used for experiments or for public entertainment.

Standing like a prehistoric monster with its feet pointing to the sky are four of the tallest chimneys in London, rising over 90 metres into the air and belonging to the former **Battersea power station** (2). The building was designed by Sir Giles Gilbert Scott (1880-1960) and erected between 1932 and 1934; the station supplied electricity for an area extending from Greenwich to Maidenhead and from Chertsey to Chesham. When the foundations were being dug, a 2000-year-old skull was found in the riverbank. There were no cooling towers because the central heating for the Pimlico Estate, on the opposite bank of the river, was supplied by pipe from the station. The station is now awaiting a new role as the centrepiece of a leisure and business development.

The station's next-door neighbour is a gasholder which also stands over 90 metres high and is capable of holding 200,000 cubic metres of gas.

Across the road from the power station is one of London's loveliest open spaces, **Battersea Park** (3), which was the work of Sir James Pennethorne (1801-71), the stepson of John Nash, who was George IV's favourite architect. There are two 'sides' to the park; one is the Festival Gardens, established here as part of the Festival of Britain in 1951; the other comprises playing fields, an English garden, a cricket ground and a fine running track. In addition there are a boating lake, flowerbeds and winding paths to intrigue visitors. Before the park was laid out, the marshland was used by market-gardeners who, it is said, first grew asparagus here. Gentlemen fought duels here, amongst them the first Duke of Wellington and the Earl of Winchelsea. The duel took place because Lord Winchelsea had accused the Duke of dishonesty in connection with the Catholic Emancipation Bill. Apparently it was the Duke's intention to fire his pistol at his opponent's legs — but he missed! Lord Winchelsea fired into the air, apologised to the Duke, and honour was satisfied — and all this at eight o'clock in the morning! At that time there were extensions being carried out to the London docks, and the earth removed from them was transported to fill in the marshland of Battersea Fields, as the area now occupied by the park was then known.

The Japanese order of Buddhist monks, Nipponzan Myohosi, erected a 'Peace Pagoda' on the river side of the park. It was officially opened on 18th May 1985.

At either end of Battersea Park are suspension bridges over the Thames. The one

Battersea Park.

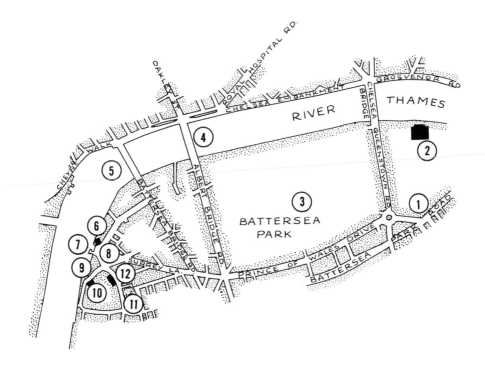

BATTERSEA

1. *Battersea Dogs' Home*	5. *Battersea Bridge*	9. *Vicarage Crescent*
2. *Battersea power station*	6. *Church of St Mary the Virgin*	10. *Old Battersea House*
3. *Battersea Park*	7. *Church Dock*	11. *Castle public house*
4. *Albert Bridge*	8. *Raven public house*	12. *Sir Walter St John School*

to the east, Chelsea Bridge, dates from 1937, when it cost £85,000. It replaced a bridge built in 1858 and which, until 1897, was a toll bridge. To the west is one of the few surviving nineteenth-century suspension bridges over the river, the **Albert Bridge** (4), which links the Chelsea Embankment, opened between 1871 and 1874, with Battersea on the south bank of the river. The bridge was opened in 1873, the work of R. M. Ordish, who also designed the roof of St Pancras station; its central span is 120 metres, although since 1973 it has been supported from underneath.

The next bridge upstream to the west is **Battersea Bridge** (5). Designed by Sir Joseph Bazalgette (1819-90), it replaces the wooden bridge built between 1771 and 1773, which has been immortalised in James McNeill Whistler's painting of it. The first Earl Spencer (1734-83) conveyed the right of the ferry here to the Battersea Bridge Company and became a director of it. The central arch, the highest of the set, allows the larger tankers and others vessels to pass through on their way up river.

The parish church of St Mary the Virgin, Battersea, and Church Dock.

The parish church of **St Mary the Virgin** (6) was rebuilt in 1777 by Jos. Dixon, who is described as being a 'builder of Westminster'. Here William Blake (1757-1827), artist, poet and mystic, married Katherine, the daughter of a market-gardener. Although unable to write her name, she 'signed' the marriage register with a cross; she was a devoted wife and Blake could not resist painting her on his deathbed. The east window comprises the finest seventeenth-century stained glass, full of heraldic devices. Possibly the work of Bernard van Linge, one of the greatest glassworkers of his time, the window is said to have come from the previous church. It was given by Sir John St John and shows his relationship with the royal house of Tudor. Included are portraits of Margaret Beauchamp, Henry VII and Elizabeth I, with their coats of arms and those of the St John family. The windows either side of the main one are eighteenth-century and the work of James Pearson. The registers, an almost complete set from 1559, contain a number of interesting entries and signatures. William Wilberforce witnessed a wedding conducted by the Reverend John Venn, Rector of Clapham; both men were founder members of the Clapham Sect, a group determined to free all slaves in the British Empire, an aim they ultimately fulfilled. There is also record of the burials of the American general Benedict Arnold on 14th June 1801 and of his wife, Margaret, on 25th August 1804. Arnold had defected to the British side during the War of American Independence, for which he and his wife both received pensions for life. J. W. M. Turner, the artist (1775-1851), used to sit in the vestry at the west end of the church to paint the sunsets over the Thames. In spite of more recent building on the other side of the river, the sunsets can still be enjoyed today. In the crypt can be seen, mounted on the walls, sixty of the lead inscriptions from the three hundred coffins once buried here. On the inside walls of the church are many memorials and monuments. On the south wall of the gallery is Sir Edward Wynter's monument from the old church. It tells how he crushed to death a tiger and overthrew sixty Moors in single conflict. In the western section of the churchyard lies buried William Curtis, who died in 1799. He was an eminent botanist, whose great contribution to horticulturists and agriculturists was his book on British grasses. He also produced an illustrated book on wild plants around London.

Just outside the west end of the churchyard is **Church Dock** (7), a local landing stage and hithe — a dock cut into the riverbank. It was here that local inhabitants would unload their goods from barges and lighters.

By the former village square, now Battersea Square, stands the **Raven public house** (8) with its seventeenth-century Dutch-style gables, a reminder that hundreds of years ago the square was a general meeting place. It is said that Charles II (1630-85) frequently used the ferry from Chelsea, where doubtless he had been to see the lovely Nell Gwynne, and visited the Raven after bathing in the river. On one occasion Colonel Thomas Blood, who achieved notoriety by trying to steal the Crown Jewels from the Tower of London, lay in wait for the king. But at the last moment he could not bring himself to kill Charles and, on confessing his crime, received a royal pardon and a pension of £500.

Leading out of the square is **Vicarage Crescent** (9), where can be found Devonshire House and the old vicarage, both of which date from the eighteenth century, reminders of the numerous similar houses which once lined the riverbank. On the wall of the old vicarage is a blue plaque recording that Edward Adrian Wilson, the famous Antarctic explorer and naturalist, lived in the house. Born at Cheltenham in 1872, he was one of the party of five who reached the South Pole on 12th January 1912. His body was found with those of Scott and Bowers after their ill-fated attempt to return to *Terra Nova*, the base ship for the expedition.

Although now cut off from the river by the road, the seventeenth-century **Old Battersea House** (10), said by some to have been designed by Sir Christopher Wren (1632-1723), is a fine building, with its

The Raven public house, Battersea.

hipped roof visible above the surrounding wall. When in the 1930s the immediate area was being redeveloped by Battersea Borough Council, Colonel and Mrs Stirling bought a life tenancy of the building, and soon the house was attracting many visitors to see their collection of Pre-Raphaelite paintings by Evelyn de Morgan, Mrs Stirling's sister, and the ceramics of William de Morgan. In addition, the Stirlings had gathered together a fine collection of seventeenth-century furniture. The lease of the house has now been acquired by the Ford Foundation of America, which has restored it to its former glory. Visits may be arranged by appointment.

Further redevelopment in the area of Battersea High Street in recent years has meant the demolition of a number of the older houses in this neighbourhood, including the sixteenth-century tavern, the **Castle** (11). However, the tavern has since been rebuilt and the original Tudor inn-sign, carved from a solid piece of wood, can now be seen outside the new house.

For the first 150 years of its existence the **Sir Walter St John School** (12) was the only school in Battersea, having been founded by the third baronet in 1700 'for the education of twenty free scholars'. It was rebuilt and enlarged in 1859 and 1915 but closed in 1988. The building now houses Thomas's Preparatory School. Over the archway into the school can be seen the arms and motto of the St John family, 'Rather deathe than false of faythe'.

The old vicarage, Battersea, once home of Edward Adrian Wilson.

2
Chelsea

It is said that Chelsea was originally called *Celchyth*, meaning a hithe (landing place) for chalk or lime, but Norden, writing in the seventeenth century, claims that it was a strand or riverside roadway, like a chesil, 'which the sea casteth up', made of sand and pebbles from the river.

Connecting the north (Chelsea) and south (Battersea) banks of the river is **Chelsea Bridge** (1), described in the chapter about Battersea. From the bridge one has a fine view of the Chelsea skyline.

Leave the bridge and make your way to the **Chelsea Embankment** (2), constructed by Sir Joseph Bazalgette, the engineer, and completed in 1871. Built into the side of the embankment is a tunnel, the present-day outlet for one of London's lost rivers, the **Westbourne** (3). This is visible from the bridge.

On the site of a monastic almshouse and theological college Charles II founded in 1682 the **Royal Hospital** (4) as a place of retirement for veteran soldiers from the recently established standing army of England. In the grounds of the Hospital the Chelsea Flower Show takes place each May. We shall visit the hospital again later on our tour of Chelsea.

Continue along the riverside to the **Chelsea Physic Garden** (5), founded in 1673 by the Society of Apothecaries of the City of London. The freehold was given to the Society by Sir Hans Sloane on condition that the gardens were kept 'for the manifestation of the glory, power and wisdom of God'. A statue of Sloane stands in the garden. It is a copy of the original by Rysbrack, which has been removed to the foyer of the British Museum. The cotton seeds used for the first cotton fields in the United States were grown here. Today the establishment is devoted to research. It is open to the public on Sunday and Wednesday afternoons.

Cheyne Walk (6) has had many distinguished residents. The novelist George Eliot (the pen name of Mary Ann Cross, née Evans) is commemorated by a blue plaque on number 4, where she moved towards the end of her life. Her next-door neighbour at number 5 was John Camden Nield, the musician, who bequeathed £500,000 to Queen Victoria. At the end of the eighteenth century an Italian doctor called Dominietti spent £37,000 in establishing a fashionable bathing centre for medicinal purposes at number 6. Number 10 was once the residence of Lloyd George and, later, of Randall Thomas Davidson, Archbishop of Canterbury from 1903 to 1928. Built in 1717, number 16 was first occupied by Robert Chapman, whose monogram RC can be seen on the wrought-iron gateway, and later by Dante Gabriel Rossetti and Algernon Charles Swinburne. James McNeill Whistler, the American artist, lived for a time at number 21. Henry VIII built a palace here but nothing of it remains above ground except a small hunting lodge in nearby Glebe Place.

Cadogan Pier (7) has been passed before we reach Rossetti's house but, looking back, both the pier and the **Albert Bridge** (8) can be seen. The annual Doggett's Coat and Badge rowing race takes place on the river here. The race was inaugurated to commemorate the accession of George I in 1714 and the establishment of the House of Hanover on the British throne. The Albert Bridge, built to the designs of R. C. Ordish and opened in 1873, is of cantilever and suspension construction. Its structure has become fragile in recent years and an additional support has been placed under the central span.

With the growth in the population of the parish in the late eighteenth and early nineteenth centuries a new church became nec-

essary. A new site was found in St Luke's Street and the old parish church of **All Saints** (9) was demoted to become a daughter church to the new one. Extensive damage by bombs in the Second World War has been repaired and the building today is a fine example of a church of the medieval and later periods. Thomas More's chapel, built for him in 1528, is a very early example of the Renaissance influence.

Opposite the west tower of the church are the **Margaret Roper Gardens** (10), made since the war and a pleasant oasis for the weary walker to rest. Margaret Roper was the daughter of Thomas More; she rescued

Left: *The Royal Hospital, Chelsea.*

Right: *Crosby Hall, Chelsea.*

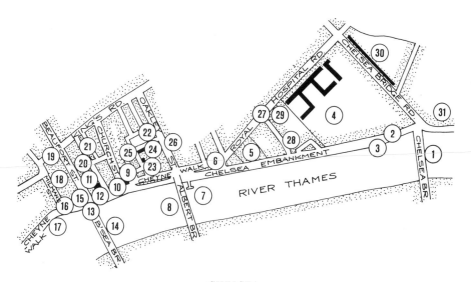

CHELSEA

1. Chelsea Bridge
2. Chelsea Embankment
3. Outlet of Westbourne
4. Royal Hospital
5. Physic Garden
6. Cheyne Walk
7. Cadogan Pier
8. Albert Bridge
9. All Saints church
10. Margaret Roper Gardens
11. Site of house of Sir John Danvers

12. Crosby Hall
13. More's Garden
14. Battersea Bridge
15. Mrs Gaskell's house
16. Lindsay House
17. River boats
18. Moravian Cemetery
19. King's Road
20. Catholic chapel
21. Paultons Square
22. Henry VIII's hunting lodge
23. Carlyle's House

24. Church of the Holy Redeemer
25. Upper Cheyne Row
26. Oakley Street
27. Tite Street
28. White House
29. National Army Museum
30. Chelsea Barracks
31. Site of Grosvenor Canal entrance

her father's head, which had been placed on top of the south gate of the City of London after his execution on Tower Hill in 1535. In 1969 Cubitt Bevis's statue of Thomas More was unveiled in front of the church.

Sir John Danvers, one of the signatories to the death warrant of Charles I, built himself a house here (11) in the seventeenth century, but nothing of it remains.

Moved to its present site in the early twentieth century, **Crosby Hall** (12) was once the home of the Crosby family. Originally built in 1466 in Bishopsgate in the City, it was dismantled because of a road-widening scheme and re-erected here. At one time Thomas More owned the house and it is appropriate that it should now stand here so near to where he lived.

On the corner of the embankment and Beaufort Street there is a block of flats called **More's Garden** (13). Look carefully at the decoration of the entrance step to see its floral tribute to Thomas's garden.

The present **Battersea Bridge** (14) was built in 1890 and replaced the eighteenth-century one. **Number 93 Cheyne Walk** (15) was the home of Mrs Gaskell, the novelist, author of *North and South* and

The memorial to Thomas More in Beaufort Street, Chelsea, with his portrait in mosaic.

Cranford, who was born here in 1810.

Most of the grand houses and palaces have long since disappeared from the Chelsea riverside but **Lindsay House** (16) survives. Built in 1674, it was originally a single three-storeyed house, but a hundred years later it was divided into three houses. Here, in the eighteenth century, came Count Zinzendorf, a great benefactor of the Moravian Church; the house became the English headquarters of the church. At number 98 lived the Brunels, civil engineers, in the nineteenth century.

Across the road from Lindsay House are moored **river boats** (17), in which people live and work, so keeping alive this portion of the river.

Retrace your steps a short way and turn left up Milman's Street; on the right will be seen Moravian Close, which leads to the **Moravian Cemetery** (18), where members of the church are buried. The plot of ground is laid out in four squares, one quarter being used for the burial of married men, another

for single men, and the other two for married and unmarried women. A small flat stone marks each grave and this led to the tradition that Moravians are buried standing up, with only one person to each grave. Permission to visit the cemetery should be obtained from the Moravian Church.

At the end of the street turn right along the **King's Road** (19), once the private road of the king, leading from Westminster to Hampton Court. Today the road is the high street of Chelsea and a centre for shopping. Beaufort Street is soon reached; walk down it towards the river and on the left-hand side you will see a large rood, or crucifix, on the outside wall of a **Catholic chapel** (20). This chapel is on the site of the house in which Thomas More lived. Down the side of the building you will see the wall of the garden of the house. Until a few years ago the house and chapel were the home of an order of Catholic nuns, but they have moved out of London and the buildings are now occupied by a seminary for Roman Catholic ordinands, Allen Hall. A mosaic on the side wall depicts the head of Thomas More.

Return to the King's Road and on the right-hand side is **Paultons Square** (21). A walk round reveals the unified pattern of the houses, built in the early nineteenth century.

Returning once more to the King's Road and passing Old Church Street and Bramerton Street, turn right into Glebe Place. At the end is the old **hunting lodge** of Henry VIII's palace (22), now used as a day nursery. Follow the street round, first to the right and then to the left. It meets Upper Cheyne Row and Cheyne Row, and at number 24 Cheyne Row is **Carlyle's House** (23), maintained by the National Trust. Here the great historian Thomas Carlyle lived for nearly fifty years. His clothes are in the wardrobe and his double-walled refuge from the noise of the town still exists. It is open to the public from April to October.

At the Glebe Place end of Cheyne Row is the Catholic **church of the Holy Redeemer and St Thomas More** (24); More's coat of arms is over the main entrance. It is sad that the church door has had to be caged in to prevent vandalism.

Walk along **Upper Cheyne Row** (25) and notice the curious numbering of the houses — there is no number 26. Was one of the occupants superstitious of double thirteen? There is a plaque to Leigh Hunt on number 22 and the delightful end house bears the date 1767.

At the end of the Row is **Oakley Street**

(26). While the buildings are not of great architectural merit, the street has a number of associations with famous people. At number 56 lived Robert Falcon Scott, the Antarctic explorer.

Turn left after leaving Upper Cheyne Row and return to the King's Road; turn right and walk along to Flood Street, on the right. Walk down this until Cheyne Walk appears on the right and Royal Hospital Road on the left. Follow the latter and soon the wall of the Physic Garden will be reached; and for another peep into the grounds turn right down Swan Walk, then follow Dilke Street into **Tite Street** (27). The artist Whistler came here in the late nineteenth century. E. W. Godwin designed the **White House**

Left: *Number 56 Oakley Street, Chelsea, home of Robert Falcon Scott.*
Right: *The statue of Thomas Carlyle in Chelsea Embankment gardens.*

(28) for him and was also responsible for the Tower House and the Studios in the same street. Another American painter, John Singer Sargent, lived at number 31 and the British artist Augustus John lived at 33. For eleven years Oscar Wilde lived at number 34, opposite which once stood the Victoria Hospital for Children, into which was incorporated Gough House, the Chelsea home of Sir Richard Gough, who gave his name to Gough Square in the City of London.

Having explored Tite Street, return to Royal Hospital Road, turn right, and the **National Army Museum** (29) is on the right-hand side. It illustrates the history of the British Army from the seventeenth century.

'Old soldiers never die, they only fade away' — so the popular song tells us, and what better place for them to fade away than at the Royal Hospital. Entrance to the buildings and grounds of the hospital is either by the Chelsea Gate, nearest to the National Army Museum, or by the London Gate at the further end of the road. It is well worth a visit, especially if you can persuade one of the pensioners to act as your guide. Do not forget to visit the tiny museum near the London Gate.

Leaving by either gate, turn right and soon you will find yourself at crossroads. Opposite are the **Chelsea Barracks** (30) of the modern army and you have a choice of going left to Sloane Square, ahead to Victoria, or right down towards the river and Chelsea Bridge again.

If you choose the last, pass the barracks on your right, and at the junction of the roads and the bridge you will find on your left the entrance to the former **Grosvenor Canal**, now used as a refuse collection point by the City of Westminster, and the pumping station for a waterworks (31).

The Albert Bridge, Battersea.

The tomb of William Hogarth in St Nicholas's churchyard, Chiswick (left), and a detail of Hogarth's tomb (inset).

Below: Chiswick Square has a plaque stating that this is the garden into which Becky Sharp throws Johnson's dictionary in Thackeray's 'Vanity Fair'.

3
Chiswick

Over the years many famous people have been attracted to live in this charming village setting alongside the river Thames. Artists and writers have come here to work and architects have added their contribution.

As in many other places the village life centres around the parish church, with the 'big house' not far away down the lane. There have been sufficient ways in and out to help transport people and goods from place to place. The eventual explosion of population came in the late eighteenth and early nineteenth centuries.

In tenth-century Anglo-Saxon charters the name is given as *Ceswican*, which means 'cheese farm', cheese presumably being a local product.

In keeping with the fashion of the time William Hogarth (1697-1764) moved out of London to Chiswick about 1749 and bought a house — **Hogarth's House** (1) — where he continued to live until his death in 1764. His widow lived on at the house, attending services at the parish church, 'a stately figure in a bath chair'.

Hogarth came from Westmorland stock. It was his father, Richard Hogarth, who left the north and came, with his family, to live in London. Originally William was bound by his father as an apprentice to a silversmith, but William had other ideas and at the end of his apprenticeship attended the school of art run by Sir James Thornhill, the famous painter. At the age of 22 he set up in business on his own, but most of his early work appears to have been engravings for bills and tradesmen's shop-window cards, samples of which still exist today. In 1729 he married Jane Thornhill, having eloped with her to Paddington Green church; the marriage was against the wishes of her father, but the men were later reconciled.

Today Hogarth's House is a museum, open to the public, and examples of his work are on display, but his finest series of paintings — *The Rake's Progress* and *The Election* — are on show at the Soane Museum in Lincoln's Inn Fields.

Opposite a modern industrial factory and alongside a very busy road, and yet holding their own against all these difficulties, stand **Boston House** and **Chiswick Square** (2). Built in the late seventeenth century, the square forms a forecourt to the house. It is into this square that Becky Sharp throws the dictionary in Thackeray's *Vanity Fair*.

Off Church Street is a private lane in which stand **Page's Yard Cottages** (3), undisturbed by the passing of time as they have been for three hundred years.

In Church Street, opposite The Old Burlington, a late medieval house once known as the Burlington Arms, are an **anchor** (4) and ship's wheel.

Peculiar to London's river are its 'eyots' — small islands — of which some are inhabited but others are resting places only for birds. **Chiswick Eyot** (5) has no regular residents but at low tide is often a source of delight to boys and girls who wade out to the island.

When William Hogarth died in 1764 at his house in Leicester Square, he was buried

Cottage in Church Street, Chiswick.

in the churchyard of St Nicholas's, the parish church of Chiswick. **Hogarth's tomb** (6), restored by a descendant, bears the following epitaph:

Farewell, great painter of mankind
Who reached the noblest point of art
Whose pictured morals charm the mind
And through the eye correct the heart.

If genius fire thee, Reader, stay
If nature touch thee, drop a tear
If neither move thee, move away
For Hogarth's honoured dust lies here.

Serving as the parish church of Chiswick as it and its predecessors have done for centuries is **St Nicholas's church** (7). All that remains of the fifteenth-century and later church is the tower, the rest having been pulled down and rebuilt in the Gothic style in 1882-4 by John Loughborough Pearson (1817-97). It is said that within the area covered by the previous church two daughters of Oliver Cromwell were buried anonymously for fear of reprisals. Cromwell's daughter Mary married the Earl of Falconberg, whose country house, Sutton Court, was in Chiswick.

St Nicholas's church and churchyard, Chiswick.

To the west of the church, in what has become Chiswick Cemetery, an extension to the former graveyard of the church, can be seen the **cenotaph** (8) (empty tomb) of the Italian patriot and poet Ugo Foscolo (1778-1827). When he died Garibaldi came and laid a wreath on his tomb. After the unification of Italy in 1871 the body was exhumed and re-interred, with all suitable honours, in Santa Croce, Florence. Today there is another inscription on the side of the former tomb, which reads: 'This spot, where for forty-four years the relics of Ugo Foscolo reposed in honoured custody, will be forever held in grateful remembrance by the Italian nations.'

Some 120 metres into the cemetery and lying alongside the wall is **Whistler's tomb** (9). James McNeill Whistler, born in 1834 at Lowell, Massachusetts, spent his later years in England, dying in London in 1903.

The name of Joseph Paxton (1801-65) is always associated with glasshouses and greenhouses; many English stately homes have conservatories designed by him. Here, within the grounds of Chiswick House, is a **greenhouse** (10) he designed. Paxton had been associated with Chiswick in his younger days as a gardener.

Although designed in the first place by Inigo Jones (1573-1652) to be the watergate for Beaufort House in Chelsea, the **Inigo Jones Gateway** (11) seems to have settled in very well in its present situation. Pope wrote:

I was brought from Chelsea last year
Batter'd with wind and weather
Inigo Jones put me together
Sir Hans Sloane let me alone
Burlington brought me hither.

James McNeill Whistler's tomb in Chiswick Cemetery.

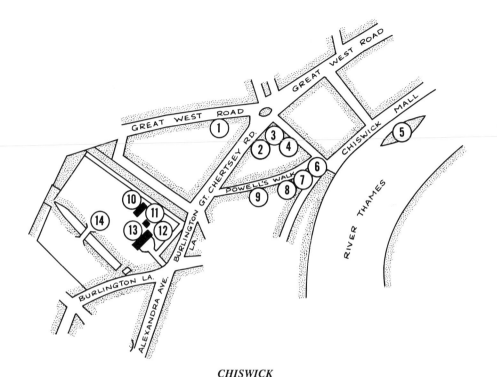

CHISWICK

1. Hogarth's House
2. Boston House and Chiswick
   Square
3. Page's Yard Cottages
4. Anchor
5. Chiswick Eyot
6. Hogarth's tomb
7. St Nicholas's church
8. Ugo Foscolo's cenotaph
9. Whistler's tomb
10. Paxton's greenhouse
11. Inigo Jones gateway
12. Site of royal gardens
13. Chiswick House
14. Chiswick House grounds

It was first erected at Chelsea in 1621 for the Duke of Beaufort.

King Edward VII (1841-1910) used to come to Chiswick House with his family during his holidays. The royal children, including the later King George V, were each allocated a small plot of land to look after. These plots (12) were behind the hedge here but have since disappeared in the replanning of the garden.

Although earlier in its history a number of famous people were associated with **Chiswick House** (13), it was not until

Richard Boyle (1695-1753), a great patron of the arts, succeeded to the title of Earl of Burlington that the villa of today became possible. After his first grand tour of Europe in 1714-15 he commissioned alterations to Burlington House in Piccadilly. However, during his visit to Italy in 1719 he acquired a fuller knowledge of architecture and in particular of the buildings of Andrea Palladio (1518-80), whose works were already known in England through Inigo Jones, the scenic designer turned architect. Palladio's Villa Capra inspired Burlington

Chiswick House.

to have built, attached to the Jacobean house here at Chiswick, a 'Temple of the Arts' in which he could keep his collection of books, manuscripts and *objets d'art*. The villa, begun in 1725 and completed in 1729, was enlarged by James Wyatt (1746-1813), came up for sale and, but for the intervention of the local and county councils, would today be a housing estate. In the period just after the Second World War the Ministry of Works and Public Buildings (now the Department of the Environment) took over the care of the villa. In its careful restoration of the villa it removed Wyatt's additions and returned the building to the appearance it had when it was first built in the early eighteenth century.

While the villa's design is the work of Lord Burlington, inspired by Palladio, the laying out of the **grounds** (14) is that of William Kent (1684-1748). This was one of the earliest garden plans to break away from the formal designs of the age of Wren and to produce an 'English garden'. Using the villa as a focus, the avenues and vistas present an example of the care and attention paid to landscaping in the eighteenth century. The cedars of Lebanon were planted, as saplings, in 1642. The classical bridge over the canal is the remaining work of James Wyatt. At various vantage points in the grounds obelisks are set up. One of these has incorporated in it a Roman tomb commemorating a husband, wife and child of the second century, which came from the Arundel Collection of marbles. Another is in a pond in the amphitheatre. There are also an Ionic temple, a Doric column and the foundations of an orangery to be found within the gardens.

The classical bridge in the gardens at Chiswick House.

Above: *The house of Sir Charles Barry on Clapham Common, now the Trinity Hospice.*
Below left: *The drinking fountain near the Children's Lido Pond on Clapham Common.*
Below right: *The wrought-iron gates of the former vicarage of St Peter's at 23 Old Town, Clapham.*

4
Clapham

Clapham, mentioned in the Domesday Survey of 1086 as *Clopeham* — 'ham' meaning homestead, and Clope or Cloppa being the family name of the Saxon inhabitants — is also taken to be 'the homestead on the hill'. The first mention of a church here is in the twelfth century; it was near to the site of the present St Paul's church in Rectory Grove. Today Clapham is a thriving inner suburb and can no longer be described as 'a village four miles from the City'. Few places more thoroughly repay the time spent on research into their past than Clapham does with its long and interesting history. Through here have passed kings and queens of England on their way from one royal palace to another; here men and women of the arts have retired, perhaps for health reasons, and spent their last days walking across Clapham Common and enjoying its peace and quiet.

Clapham Common today covers an area of 83 hectares and there are four ponds for water enthusiasts to enjoy. The **Eagle Pond** (1), now used by fishermen and birds, gets its name from the eagles on a house, which has long since disappeared, in nearby Narbonne Avenue. On the **Long Pond** (3) model boatmen can try their skills against the wind and weather. It was originally called the Boathouse Pond because the lord of the manor maintained a boathouse here. The **Children's Lido Pond** (7), near the parish church, was once known as the Cock Pond, after the tavern opposite. It is also shown on maps as the Pound or Pit Pond because it came into being in the late eight-

eenth century as a result of quarrying for soil and gravel to raise the site of the new parish church. Close by is a splendid drinking fountain erected by the temperance movement, topped with a figure of a woman giving a drink to an old man.

On the south side of the common are a small oasis of houses and the **Windmill public house** (2). The inn sign today shows a picture of the post mill which may well be the one referred to in seventeenth-century documents and from which the inn gets its name. The Windmill dates from the eighteenth century and was the recognised starting point for local horse races over the common. The parish register of the early eighteenth century records that the vestry meetings were held at the Cock, the Plough and the Windmill inns.

The **milestone** (4) on Clapham Common South Side, near the junction with Rookery Road, reads 'Royal Exchange 4½ miles' (on the east and west faces) and 'Whitehall 4 miles' (on the south). The north side is defaced.

The Catholic church of Clapham is **St Mary's** (5), which was built in 1851. When it was decided in the 1930s to build a new parish hall, the site in St Alphonsus Road was chosen. In digging for the foundations remains were found of a plague or pest hospice on the site. It was not uncommon in times of pestilence for small 'villages' to be created outside established towns, away from the general population of the area. This was one of them.

The nineteenth-century historian and man

Holy Trinity church on Clapham Common.

of letters, Thomas, Lord Macaulay (1800-59), lived at **5 The Pavement** (6), as did his father Zachary Macaulay, the philanthropist and campaigner for the abolition of the slave trade. A stone plaque today marks the house, which was described by Thomas as being 'a roomy, comfortable dwelling, with a small garden behind'.

Near to the area of the Old Town known as the Polygon is the nineteenth-century fire station (8). Its modern counterpart can be seen further round in Old Town, Clapham, close to number 23 Old Town (10).

The architect of Westminster Cathedral, John Bentley, lived at **43 Old Town** (9), the end house of a charming row dating from the time of Queen Anne. A blue commemorative plaque now distinguishes this house from others in the terrace. Bentley came to live here in 1894, the year work started on

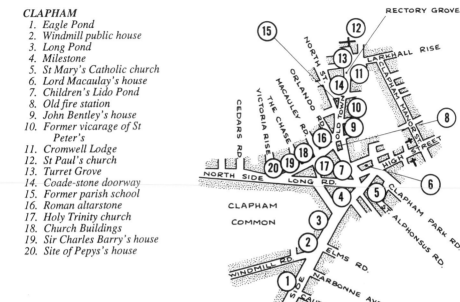

the cathedral, and died here on 2nd March 1902. He is buried at Mortlake Cemetery.

At **23 Old Town** (10) can be seen an eighteenth-century house, the former vicarage of St Peter's church, Clapham Manor Street, with its original wrought-iron railings. Had it not been for the persistence of a former vicar, the Reverend A. J. W. Pritchard, these valuable railings would have ended up during the Second World War as scrap iron. Returning home one day, with a preservation order in his pocket, Mr Pritchard found workmen already removing the railings. On production of the necessary documents work ceased and the railings were stored safely in the vicarage until the end of the war. The house is now used by the Sisters of the Anglican Order of St Margaret.

Cromwell Lodge (11) is the name given to the house in Rectory Grove almost opposite St Paul's church, because, it is said, Oliver Cromwell used it as a hideaway.

When the new church was built on the common, **St Paul's** (12), the original parish church, was allowed to fall into disrepair. However, with the growth of the area in the early nineteenth century, it was rebuilt and a number of the treasures from the earlier church were restored. 'A diligent, faithful and esteemed servant of Charles II and James II' is an apt description of William Hewer, whose memorial can be seen in the church. He was the great friend and partner of Samuel Pepys and it was to Hewer's house at Clapham that Pepys retired in 1700 and where he died in 1703.

Turret Grove (13), near which the manor house once stood, is a reminder of the great Elizabethan mansion, which has long since disappeared, except, it is said, for the foundation of the turret that gives the street its name.

The entrance doorway of **52 Rectory Grove** (14) is made of Coade stone and is very reminiscent of Portland Place in Marylebone.

The local **parish school** (15) was founded here in 1648 but has outgrown the site and been rebuilt in Victoria Rise, off the North Side, Clapham Common.

In the forecourt of the local branch library is a **Roman altarstone** (16). Found in the grounds of Cavendish House around 1900, it was presented to the library by Councillor Golds and is believed to date from the first century.

On the south-west corner of **Holy Trinity church** (17), 'the church on the common', can be found the war-scarred memorial stone to the Clapham Sect. This was a group of gentlemen from the parish who led the successful fight against slavery in the British Empire, who 'laboured so abundantly for

The milestone on Clapham Common.

national righteousness and the conversion of the heathen and rested not until the curse of slavery was swept away from all parts of the British Dominions'. The inscription goes on to list Charles Grant, Zachary Macaulay, Granville Sharp, John Shore, James Stephens, Henry and John Thornton, Henry and John Venn and William Wilberforce. The memorial was unveiled in 1919.

Opposite the west end of Holy Trinity church are the **Church Buildings** (18), which are said to have been designed by Sir Christopher Wren between 1713 and 1720. Captain Cook, the eighteenth-century explorer of Australia and New Zealand, lived in Clarence House while the house to the left is supposed to be Clapham Academy, where Thomas Hood went to school and about which he wrote an 'Ode on a Distant Prospect of Clapham Academy', with its painful memories.

Sir Charles Barry, architect of the Houses of Parliament, lived from 1850 to 1860 in a house on the North Side, Clapham Common (19). Today it is the Trinity Hospice. Founded in 1891 as a refuge for the dying, it was run by the Order of St Margaret of East Grinstead from 1895 until 1977, when the council appointed a management team. In 1980 the name changed to the Trinity Hospice.

The hospice stands on ground that was once part of the gardens of the house in which the seventeenth-century diarist Samuel Pepys lived for the last years of his life. It was called **The Great House** (20) but has long since disappeared. Here Pepys died in 1703; he was buried in St Olave's church, Hart Street, in the City of London. John Evelyn, another diarist of the period, records how he visited Pepys at Clapham and found the house to be useful and capacious.

5
Clerkenwell

One of London's most intriguing villages, Clerkenwell takes its name from the Worshipful Company of Parish Clerks of the City of London, who performed their annual mystery plays close to the well here.

In 1863 **Farringdon underground station** (1) was built as the terminus of the first route of London's underground railway system. The line ran from Bishop's Bridge Road (Paddington) to this station.

Outside the station turn left to the **Castle public house** (2), at number 34 Cowcross Street. The signboard displays the usual castle but also the three brass balls of the pawnbroker. It is the only public house in Britain that has a pawnbroker's licence. George IV, while still the Prince of Wales, visited a nearby cock-fight and lost heavily with his bets until all that he had left was a watch, given to him by his father, George III. He persuaded the landlord to pawn his watch in return for five pounds and, his luck having changed, was able to redeem his watch later without telling the licensee his identity. He later sent him a licence to act officially as a pawnbroker, hence the double signboard for the house.

Walk along Cowcross Street, its title reminding us of the close proximity of Smithfield Market and in former times the abattoirs, until **Peter's Lane** (3) is reached on the left-hand side of the roadway. Walk up the lane until St John Street and St John's Lane are reached. It was from this spot that between 1612 and 1780 distances along the Great North Road were measured.

From this junction of roads follow St John's Lane to **St John's Gatehouse** (4), the sole remaining feature, above ground, of the original buildings of the Order of St John of Jerusalem, the Knights Hospitallers. Founded in the twelfth century with the object of defending places in the Holy Land from attacks by the Saracens, the order became one of the wealthiest and most powerful in Europe until it was disbanded at the time of the Reformation in the sixteenth century. The gatehouse was sacked by Wat Tyler in his rebellion of 1381, when the rebels dragged the prior, Sir Robert Hales, into the courtyard and executed him. It was rebuilt in 1504 by Prior Thomas Docwra, while tradition says that Henry VIII courted Anne Boleyn here while he was still married to Catharine of Aragon. Later occupants of the building include the printer and publisher of the *Gentleman's Magazine*, who, not entitled to have a personal coat of arms on the side of his carriage, had the gatehouse painted on instead. Today the building, together with its nineteenth-century additions, houses the Order of St John and its excellent **museums** (5), containing the memorabilia of the St John's Ambulance Brigade and the Order of St John of Malta.

Continue along St John's Lane and cross Clerkenwell Road and **the church of the Order of St John** (6) can be seen. Heavily bombed in the Second World War, the church has been restored to be used as both church and meeting hall for the order. In the crypt of the church can be seen the twelfth-century fabric of the previous building. Note

St John's Gatehouse and the entrance to the Museum of the Order of St John, Clerkenwell.

CLERKENWELL
1. *Farringdon station*
2. *Castle public house*
3. *Peter's Lane*
4. *St John's Gatehouse*
5. *Museum of the Order of St John*
6. *St John's church*
7. *Jerusalem Passage*
8. *Clerkenwell Green*
9. *Former Middlesex Sessions House*
10. *Marx Memorial Library*
11. *St James's church*
12. *Hugh Myddleton School*
13. *Records Office*
14. *London Spa public house*
15. *Holy Redeemer church*
16. *Finsbury Health Centre*
17. *Spa Fields*
18. *Farringdon Road*
19. *Clerks' Well*
20. *St John's Gardens*

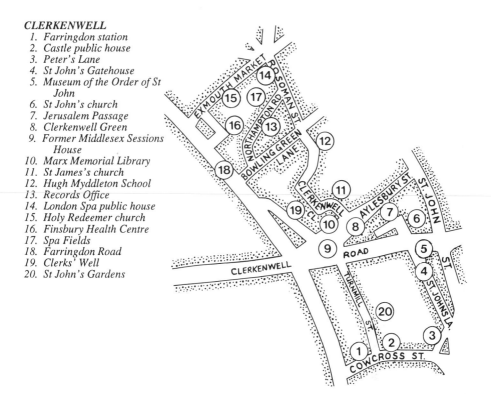

the pattern of the cobblestones in front of the church building forming part of a circle. This outlines the site of the rotunda of the twelfth-century church, which was demolished at the time of Henry VIII's Reformation. Leave the square in front of the church by **Jerusalem Passage** (7).

The Passage is a pleasant pedestrian way leading to Aylesbury Street. At its junction is a plaque recording the house of Thomas Britton, the musical coal merchant (1644-1714). Music lovers came from all over London to enjoy the concerts that he arranged in his house. Here George Frederick Handel often played his own compositions and those of others.

Turn left along Aylesbury Street to **Clerkenwell Green** (8), where the Artful Dodger in *Oliver Twist* gave his new pupils lessons in pickpocketing. At the far end of the Green can be seen the former **Middlesex Sessions House** (9), which was built in 1782 as a court of law. It is now a masonic conference centre, open on application. Izaak Walton (1593-1683) lived at Clerkenwell Green and here wrote *The Compleat Angler*. At 37a Clerkenwell Green, on the north side of the Green, is the **Marx Memorial Library** (10), founded in 1933. It was here that Lenin wrote his books between the years 1902 and 1903, before he moved south of the river to

Wall plaque in Jerusalem Passage, Clerkenwell, marking the site of the house of Thomas Britton.

martyrs who were burned at Smithfield in Mary Tudor's reign.

Leave the churchyard by the gate with the tower on your left and turn right to follow Clerkenwell Close. On the right, before reaching Bowling Green Lane, is the **Hugh Myddleton School** (12). This is the site of the former Mulberry Garden pleasure gardens. The land was later used as a drill

The parish church of St James, Clerkenwell.

Clapham. The building was originally erected in 1737 as a Welsh charity school and was later used as the headquarters of the London Patriotic Club from 1872 to 1892. The Twentieth Century Press used the premises until 1922.

From the Green, Clerkenwell Close leads to the 'new' parish church, designed and built by James Carr between 1788 and 1792. **St James's church** (11) is on the site of the medieval nunnery which was founded by Jordan de Briset on land adjoining the Clerks' Well. In the churchyard, against the south wall of the church, is the tombstone of Ellen Lefevre and her four children, all of whom were murdered by their father. The nunnery, which was occupied by nuns of the Benedictine Order, was suppressed in 1539 by Henry VIII. The church contains a fine organ and a memorial to the Protestant ground for the Clerkenwell Volunteers and then a house of detention was built on part of the site. From it Irishman Michael Barrett was taken in 1864 to be the last person to be hanged in public, outside Newgate Prison, Old Bailey. His fellow countrymen had attempted to free him by detonating a bomb close to the wall of the prison. The cells are still intact, beneath the school playground. The present building dates from 1893 and houses the Kingsway-Princeton College of Further Education and the Central London Institute. Note the different entrances for boys and girls over the archways of the school.

Across the road from the school is Rosoman Street, where in 1760 was opened Jackson's Grand Grotto Gardens and Gold and Silver Fish Repository. Nearby, at 40 Northampton Road, is the **Greater London Records Office** (13), which holds the records of the former Greater London Council and its predecessor, the London County Council.

On the corner of Rosoman Street and Exmouth Market is the **London Spa public house** (14), which marks the site of an old inn called the Fountain. In 1685 a spring was discovered here, and it was afterwards known as the London Spa although it never attracted the attention of the fashionable people who frequented the Islington Spa at that time. From after 1753 the London Spa seems to have been frequented only as a tavern.

One of the architects of the Arts and Crafts movement of the 1880s, John Sedding, designed the **church of the Holy Redeemer** (15) in Exmouth Market. It stands on the site of Ducking Pond House, a wayside inn that had ponds at the rear for duck hunting. These premises were bought by Thomas Rosoman, who built Sadler's

Wells theatre in 1765.

Continue to walk down Exmouth Market and shortly after the Holy Redeemer church is Pine Street. Here the **Finsbury Health Centre** (16) was erected in 1938. The design by Lebetkin and Tecton was considered revolutionary at that time.

Behind the Centre and stretching behind the entire length of Exmouth Market are **Spa Fields** (17), a reminder of the London Spa and now a public open space.

Retrace your steps to the Finsbury Health Centre and take Vineyard Walk to **Farringdon Road** (18). This road leads into the City of London, at whose boundary it becomes Farringdon Street. (There are no *roads* in the City of London.) Here are *The Guardian* newspaper's offices. The road divides at the Betsey Trotwood and the left-hand fork becomes Farringdon Lane. Here can be found at number 14/16 the **Clerks' Well** (19), which gives its name to the area that we are exploring. The well was first mentioned by Fitzstephen, in an appendix to his biography of St Thomas Becket in 1174. It had for a long time been lost sight of but was uncovered during excavations under the present buildings. Further and more recent restoration of the well has taken place and it can now be seen from a viewing and exhibition centre. Further down Farringdon Road can be found several second-hand book stalls from Monday to Saturday.

Passing behind the former Middlesex Sessions House, cross over Clerkenwell Road to Turnmill Street, the line of which follows that of the underground railway as well as the river Fleet. Shortly before reaching Cowcross Street again is found Benjamin Street, where the former burial ground of St John's church has been laid out as a pleasant **public garden** (20).

6
Dulwich

It is easy to feel that one is in the country in Dulwich — 'the village in the valley' — with all the hustle and bustle of the busy metropolis left behind in the main roads that surround the estate. The earliest record of this village is in an Anglo-Saxon charter of King Edgar (944-75), when the spelling was given as *Dilwihs*, which probably meant a place where a white flower grows in a damp meadow.

Near **West Dulwich station** (1) is Glazebrook Close, the site until 1954 of the last remaining smallholding of the village. Turn right and walk along Thurlow Park Road. Lord Chancellor Edward Thurlow, who held office in 1778 and 1783, bought land on the estate in the eighteenth century.

The table of tolls charged at the tollgate in College Road, Dulwich.

Shortly on the left-hand side of the road there is a public **car park** (2). Be warned, however, that the gates are locked when the park is closed for the night.

At the crossroads the road becomes Dulwich Common, a name that recalls that there was once a large stretch of common land here, where highwaymen used to lurk. At one time the land was a royal hunting ground used by Charles I and his court. The residents of the time were ordered by royal warrant not to hunt the king's 'stagges with greyhounds, hounds, gunnes, or any other means whatever'. Many duels were fought on the common.

The grounds and buildings of **Dulwich College** (3) are along the right-hand side of the road, the playing fields coming into view first, with the new extensions of the college beside them. The college was founded in 1619 by Edward Alleyn, a contemporary of Shakespeare and considered to be one of the finest actors of his time, on a site at the junction of Gallery and College Roads (16). Called originally Alleyn's College of God's Gift, it moved to its present site in 1870. The new college was designed by Sir Charles Barry.

The college and grounds stretch along the road towards the tollgate, past the **village pond** (4), which once served one of the two mills of Dulwich. **Pond Cottages** (5) stand behind with their weatherboarding and white-fenced front gardens. (The other mill disappeared in the late nineteenth century and stood where the north block of the college is today.)

DULWICH

1. West Dulwich station (BR)	8. Cox's Walk	15. Dulwich Picture Gallery
2. Car park	9. St Peter's church	16. Old College and
3. Dulwich College	10. Grove Tavern	almshouses
4. Village pond	11. Dulwich Park	17. Milestone and signpost
5. Pond Cottages	12. Old Burial Ground	18. Old Grammar School
6. Tollgate	13. Crown and Greyhound	19. Belair House
7. Dulwich Woods	14. Bell Cottage and other houses	20. River Effra

Continue along College Road to the last remaining operational **tollgate** in London (6), with Hunts Slip Road to the right for those vehicle owners not wishing to pay the toll and content to take the long way round to Sydenham Hill. The College Road tollgate table of charges makes interesting reading, with allowances for horses, mules, donkeys and a variety of other beasts. The tolls collected are used for the upkeep of the road, which was first made in 1789 by John Morgan of Penge, who had rented the land from the estate and needed a properly made-up road. After his death the college retained the tollgate.

Passing through the gates (there is no toll for pedestrians), the road leads towards Sydenham Hill, from where there is a good view over London from some 90 metres above sea level. **Dulwich Woods** (7) are reached and a pleasant diversion may be had by wandering through this area of 4 hectares, which is jointly managed by the London Borough of Southwark and the Dulwich College Estate. Here are playing fields, a golf course and a wild strip running along the line of the old Crystal Palace High Level Railway, which used this route between 1865 and 1954. The overgrown track leads to Cox's Walk and to the point where the railway disappears into the tunnel of Peckarman's Wood. Only householders of the Dulwich College estate can obtain the key to the nearby woods, which are private to the estate.

Cox's Walk (8), leading down the hill towards the parish church of St Peter, takes its name either from David Cox, the painter, who lived near Dulwich Ponds, or from Francis Cox, tenant of the Green Man, who had the privilege of cutting a path through the trees here.

At the foot of the lane is **St Peter's church** (9), which was built to the designs of Charles Barry Junior in 1874, on a site given by Dulwich College. Francis Bumpus, the well known writer on church architecture, served here as a choirboy. Across the road is the **Grove Tavern** (10), shown in a lease of 1732 as the Green Man and granted to Francis Cox. It once had as its neighbour the Dulwich Wells, opened in 1739, whose waters were highly recommended for their medicinal value by the doctors of the day. Their existence is known from earlier days. In the entry in his diary for 5th August 1677, John Evelyn records: 'I went this evening to visit my Lo: Brounker now taking the waters at Dullage.'

It is a short walk from the tavern to the entrance to **Dulwich Park** (11), and there are a number of interesting houses to see along the way. The park covers some 29 hectares and is now owned by the local authority but was part of the Dulwich College estate before it was handed over to the public in 1885. There is an unrivalled collection of rhododendrons and azaleas in the park, a lake on which can be seen a variety of wildfowl, an aviary and a nature trail, as well as playing fields, tennis courts and a putting green. Modern art is represented by a piece of sculpture by the late Barbara Hepworth called 'Divided Circle'.

Leave the park by the north gate, opposite Eynella (almost an anagram of Alleyn) Road and walk to the left along Court Lane, a reminder of the Dulwich court where the steward of the estate would adjudicate on local problems and misdemeanours. Soon the junction with Dulwich Village, the

The Crown and Greyhound, Dulwich.

former Dulwich High Street, and Calton Avenue is reached and the **Old Burial Ground** (12) can be seen on the left through the iron railings. Calton Avenue takes its name from the London goldsmith who sold the estate to Edward Alleyn. Facing you, in Calton Avenue, is an inscription by the road, taken from the site of the village stocks and cage, which reads: 'It is a sport for a fool to do mischief. Thine own wickedness shall correct thee.' Through the railings of the burial ground one can see the names of the families who lived here in the eighteenth and nineteenth centuries. Edward Alleyn gave the site to the villagers as their own burial ground at a time when there was no local parish church for the parishioners, only the college chapel.

Walking down the village street, one soon reaches the **Crown and Greyhound public house** (13) on the left-hand side of the road. Originally the Greyhound stood on the other side of the road but when that side was developed in 1898 it was joined to the Crown. Charles Dickens was an occasional visitor to the Dulwich Club, whose head-quarters the tavern became. The club is a social one for the Fellows of the college and principal local residents and used to meet three times a year for dinner at the Greyhound and once a year at the Ship in Greenwich, when the main toast of the evening was always 'the hamlet of Dulwich and the ladies thereof'. It still meets, but no longer at the Greyhound.

The strips of grass guarded by white posts and chains are verges previously known as 'manor wastes' which were common ground for grazing cattle. Between the Greyhound and the Old College there are a number of interesting **eighteenth-century houses** (14), particularly Bell Cottage with its weather-boarded frontage.

The road branches at the old signpost. Take the left-hand fork, College Road, cross over and enter the forecourt of the **Dulwich Picture Gallery** (15). Edward Alleyn, who was the founder of the college, made the first bequest of pictures to the college in 1626, which was followed in 1687 by the Cartwright Bequest, but it was not until the nineteenth century that a permanent gallery was built for the sole purpose of displaying the pictures accumulated by the college. Noel Desenfans, commissioned by the king of Poland to collect paintings for a royal Polish collection found himself in possession of a number of paintings when the king abdicated. Desenfans left the pictures to his wife for her pleasure during her lifetime and then, under the terms of a trust, they reverted to the Master, Warden and Fellows of Alleyn's College of God's Gift. With three collections of pictures, the Master and Fellows decided that a separate building was needed to house them. Sir John Soane (1753-1837), the architect, was commissioned to design the building, which

was completed by 1814 and opened to the public, at first free of charge, from 1817. It contains many fine paintings by Thomas Gainsborough, Peter Lely, Nicolas Poussin, Rembrandt, Joshua Reynolds, Peter Paul Rubens and many other artists. Attached to the gallery, and viewable from within the building, is the mausoleum containing the coffins of Sir Francis Bourgeois, Noel Desenfans and his wife. Before leaving the gallery the visitor should find picture number 318, 'Mrs Siddons as the Tragic Muse' by Sir Joshua Reynolds, which was used as a model by the sculptor Chavalliaud when carving the statue of Sarah Siddons that stands on Paddington Green.

In the gallery grounds is a telephone box, one of the familiar old K2 type designed by Sir Giles Gilbert Scott and introduced in 1927. Scott based his design upon the exterior of Soane's mausoleum. The kiosk was presented by British Telecom and has its original fittings.

After leaving the gallery turn left back towards Dulwich Village and shortly on the left-hand side of the road are the **Old College and almshouses** (16), which formed part of the original college and foundation. The chapel was consecrated by the seventy-fifth Archbishop of Canterbury, George Abbot, in 1616 and is still used today for Sunday services, at which members of the public are welcome. Here were to be found the Master, Warden, four fellows, twelve poor scholars, six poor brethren and six poor sisters. Today there are twelve almshouses (flats) on the east side of the building. Within the chapel lie the remains of Edward Alleyn, in a tomb in front of the altar, while over the doorway there is a Latin inscription which reads 'Blessed is he who has taken pity on the poor. Go thou and do likewise.'

Leaving the Old College buildings behind and walking through the small but pleasant garden in front of them, one arrives at the junction of College Road, Gallery Road and Dulwich Village. Here stand one of the eighteenth-century **milestones** (17), set up in 1772 by the Surveyor of the Highways, and a signpost. The worn inscription on the stone reads *Siste viator* (Rest, traveller). Just beyond are a fountain and water trough for horses, a reminder of the need in the eighteenth and nineteenth centuries to provide water for both man and beast. They are a memorial to Dr Webster, the local practitioner for some sixty years in the nineteenth century.

Turn left and walk along Gallery Road. The first building on the right-hand side of the road is the **Old Grammar School** (18). The present building was built to the designs of Sir Charles Barry, architect of the Houses of Parliament, between 1841 and 1884 as an additional school for about sixty boys. Later the school moved to larger premises in Townley Road and was named Alleyn's School. Today the building is used as a nursery school.

The route down Gallery Road leads to the rear of the Picture Gallery, to another view of the mausoleum of the founders and to a small collection of playing fields that add to the rural atmosphere of this village.

Alleyn's Cricket Ground is soon followed by Lloyd's Register Cricket Ground, and then, on the right-hand side of the road, by the entrance to Belair Park and **Belair House** (19). The grounds used to be a private estate but since 1938 have been publicly owned and managed by the local authority. The great house was possibly built to the designs of Robert Adam (1728-92) and was a private house until the beginning of the Second World War. When the borough bought the building and the land they renovated the house and, when it is not open to the public, a glimpse through the windows reveals some of the glory of this lovely eighteenth-century building.

The grounds of Belair House are open to the public and are an enchanting example of the landscaping of the eighteenth century. There is a lake fed by the **river Effra** (20), which once flowed through here on its way to the Thames near Vauxhall. This is the only part of the river that is visible above ground today. Within the park are some very fine trees and near the house there is a rare cork tree, while the wildlife includes swans, ducks and moorhens.

After the walk around the park, it is only a short way to West Dulwich station.

The Old Grammar School, Dulwich.

Dulwich Picture Gallery and the Old College.

The almshouses of Dulwich Old College.

7
Fulham

The earliest mention of the village of Fulham is in a grant of the manor to Waldhere, Bishop of London from AD 693 to 705, from Tyrhtilus, Bishop of Hereford 688-710, about the year 704, and it is then called *Fulanham*. In his book *Britannia*, the antiquarian writer William Camden (1551-1623) called it Fulham, *Volucrum Domus* — home of birds, or where birds live. Other dictionaries translating the Saxon word describe it as meaning 'Foulham', because of the alleged dirtiness of the place, or as coming from the Anglo-Saxon legal word *ful*, meaning a burial place for criminals, in which case the *ham*, homestead, must have been added later.

Overlooking the river at the north end of Putney Bridge stands the parish church of Fulham, **All Saints** (1), with its fifteenth-

The tombstone of Isabella Murr in Fulham churchyard.

century tower built of Kentish ragstone, the only surviving part of the church which stood here during the middle ages. The rest of the church was pulled down and rebuilt to the designs of Arthur Blomfield (1829-99) in the 1880s. The date of the consecration was 9th July 1881, and the reredos was added to the high altar by Heaton, Butler and Bayne in 1885. There are a number of items from the previous church, including the font, which dates from 1622, and some of the monuments. One of these, to Dorothy Clarke who died in 1695, is the work of Grinling Gibbons (1648-1721). Parts of the organ case are made up of the late seventeenth-century pulpit.

As the church is close to Fulham Palace, the former home of the Bishops of London, it is hardly surprising that there are a number of their tombs in the churchyard. One, of Bishop Thomas Sherlock (1678-1761), under the east window of the church, is signed by John Vardy. Also in the churchyard, opposite the north door, is the grave of Mr and Mrs Murr; the latter died on 29th November 1820 and her epitaph reads:

Ye who possess the brightest charms of life,
A tender friend, a kind indulgent wife,
Oh learn their worth! In her beneath this stone
These pleasant attributes shone.
Was not true happiness with them combin'd?
Ask the spoiled being she's left behind.

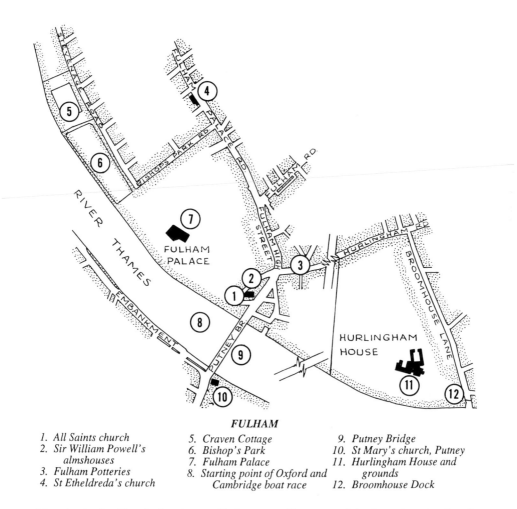

FULHAM

1. All Saints church
2. Sir William Powell's almshouses
3. Fulham Potteries
4. St Etheldreda's church
5. Craven Cottage
6. Bishop's Park
7. Fulham Palace
8. Starting point of Oxford and Cambridge boat race
9. Putney Bridge
10. St Mary's church, Putney
11. Hurlingham House and grounds
12. Broomhouse Dock

After the death of her husband was added: 'He's gone too.'

Adjacent to the churchyard, on the north side, are **Sir William Powell's almshouses** (2) for twelve poor widows. Founded in nearby Back Lane in 1680, the former premises were sold by auction in 1870, when the present buildings were built. Architecturally they are neo-Gothic in style and match in well with the design of the parish church. Notice the inscription 'God's providence, our inheritance' on the church gate end of the building.

Founded between 1672 and 1673, the **Fulham Potteries** (3) owe their existence to John Dwight of Oxfordshire, about whose earlier life little is known save the fact that he served the Bishops of Chester between 1661 and 1671. In the latter year he patented his experiments with clay and other mineral substances (patent number 164 of 1671) and moved to Fulham from Wigan —

at that time a favourite palace of the Bishops of Chester — and set up his pottery here. A number of interesting items, the work of John Dwight, are now in the Victoria and Albert Museum, South Kensington, including a beautiful half-length figure of a lifeless female child — Lydia Dwight, his daughter, who died in 1673, aged six. John Dwight was born about 1640, died in 1703 and was buried in Fulham churchyard. John Doulton, who founded the Lambeth Pottery, served his apprenticeship here. A preserved bottle oven stands by the road.

A contrast to the old parish church, **St Etheldreda's church**, Fulham Palace Road (4), was rebuilt in 1958, following the bombing in the Second World War of the Victorian church. It is smaller than its predecessor and was designed by Guy Briscoe.

The bottle oven at the Fulham Potteries.

The larger-than-life crucifix over the altar, carved by Rita Lang, is made of wood from Brighton Pier. The font is made of copper and the baptistery window, designed by Cater Shopland, shows Christ in glory in the centre, with the side lights showing the Sacraments in their biblical context and their modern counterparts.

Craven Cottage (5) was considered the prettiest specimen of cottage architecture in the early years of the nineteenth century. Built originally by the Margravine of Anspach when she was Countess of Craven, the interior offered its visitors architecture 'out of this world', with a Gothic dining room of very considerable dimensions. Sir Edward Bulwer-Lytton (1803-73), the novelist and statesman, lived here for a time and here wrote three of his novels, including *The Last of the Barons*. The site where the cottage stood became the ground of Fulham Football Club which perpetuated the name of Craven Cottage.

Originally **Bishop's Park** (6) was part of the private grounds surrounding Fulham Palace, which as early as the sixteenth century had become famous for the culture of rare and exotic plants and trees. Elizabeth I was pleased to receive from Edmund Grindal, Bishop of London 1559-70, gifts of fruit picked in these gardens. Later, in the seventeenth century, Henry Compton, Bishop 1675-1713, found great solace here during his banishment from London by James II. Doubtless his talents and inspiration were conveyed to Mary II and Anne, to whom he had been tutor, for both of these queens were enthusiastic gardeners. John Evelyn, the diarist and a great authority on trees, used to visit the gardens. On 11th October 1681 he wrote: 'I went to Fulham to visit the Bishop of London in whose garden the Sedum arborescens was in flower, which was exceeding beautiful.' Today the gardens form part of a very pleasant riverside public park.

Almost within the shadow of the parish church's tower stands **Fulham Palace** (7), the former residence of the Bishops of London. After the grant of the manor of Fulham to the Bishop of London about 794 the manor house became the country residence of the Bishops. For nearly thirteen hundred years it remained their palace, until in 1975 it was leased to the local council and a house in Westminster became London House. The moat, filled in in 1921, was nearly one mile in length and is said to have been built by a Danish army which once camped at Fulham. During the seventeenth century a sluice was constructed in order to cleanse the moat from time to time by allowing water in from the tidal river Thames. All that remains above ground today of the medieval manor house is the Great Hall of 1480 with its original timber roof. The rest of the courtyard and porch were added in the early sixteenth century and are typical Tudor buildings. Two famous bishops of the English Reformation are closely associated with the hall. Bishop Edmund Bonner tried heretics here in the sixteenth century; it is said that the Pope wished to throw him into a cauldron of molten lead. Bishop Nicholas Ridley was himself burnt as a heretic in 1555. On the north side of the courtyard is Bishop Bonner's bedroom, said to be haunted by his ghost. In the nineteenth century the hall was converted into a chapel but in 1867 the Victorian architect William Butterfield (1814-1900) built the present chapel. The east window is a memorial to Bishop William Wand's son, who was killed in a climbing accident in the Alps in 1934. The palace now houses a museum.

Every year the eyes of the public, particularly the rowing world, are focused on two

Fulham Palace: the garden façade, c.1814.

stake-boats in the river near Putney Bridge, for this is the **starting point of the Oxford and Cambridge boat race** (8). The first race was rowed in 1829 over a course at Henley-on-Thames, Oxfordshire, but it was transferred in 1845 to its present course of 4¼ miles (6.8 km) from Putney to Mortlake.

Before 1729, when the first Fulham bridge was erected linking Putney, on the south (Surrey) side of the river, with Fulham, on the north (Middlesex) side, the Bishops of London owned the ferry which plied between the two banks of the river. In 1671 the first attempt was made to erect a bridge from Fulham to Putney, but the necessary parliamentary bill was defeated by 67 votes to 54. Eventually, however, parliamentary approval was gained, and the story of the bill's passage through Parliament has been preserved for us in Anchitelle Grey's *Debates of the House of Commons*, published in 1769. In consequence of the closure of the ferry, the Bishops, their families and dependants were allowed to use the bridge free of toll. The password used was 'bishop', and it was not unusual to hear bricklayers, carpenters and others call out the word when going to the Bishop's palace on their lawful duty.

Putney Bridge (9) replaced the old Fulham Bridge of 1729 and was opened in 1884. The noted civil engineer Joseph Bazalgette designed the present bridge, which took four years to build and cost £23,975.

From the time of William the Conqueror (1027-87) until the time of the Reformation in the sixteenth century the manor of Putney was held by the Archbishops of Canterbury and had a chapel of ease to Wimbledon. Rebuilt in the fifteenth century, **St Mary's church, Putney** (10), was demolished, except for the tower and the Bishop West

Chapel, in the early nineteenth century. Several monuments from the old church were transferred to the new building. At this time the Bishop West Chapel (West was Bishop of Ely from 1515 to 1534) was left intact and is a good example of a late Gothic fan-vaulted building. In 1973 the entire interior of the church was gutted by fire, but it has now been restored. During the Civil War in the seventeenth century Generals Fairfax, Fleetwood, Ireton and Rich held a council of war sitting round the communion table of the church — wearing their hats!

Although today polo is no longer played at **Hurlingham** (11), the name continues to be associated with the sport by its followers. The Prince and Princess of Wales, later King Edward VII and Queen Alexandra, together with the Duke and Duchess of Edinburgh, were among the spectators at the first polo match played here, in 1874.

In 1760 the Bishop of London, Thomas Sherlock, gave permission to William Cadogan, a physician 'well-known in his profession', to build himself a new house in 3.6 hectares of land. The centrepiece of the present **Hurlingham House** was Dr Cadogan's 'cottage'; the rest of the building was added in the late eighteenth century by John Ellis.

According to tradition, Charles I (1600-49) used the ferry across the Thames from **Broomhouse Dock** (12) to the Feathers at Wandsworth. If the story is true, then he risked his life in doing so, for there are several recorded incidents of persons being found drowned, washed up in the dock. Broomhouse itself, described as being a little village by the riverbank in 1705, derives its name from the Anglo-Saxon word *brom*, meaning 'broom' or 'furze', which grew here abundantly at one time.

8
Greenwich

To arrive at Greenwich by river is to arrive in the time-honoured way, as thousands of noble lords, with their ladies, have done in past times. It requires a little imagination today to think of the pleasant countryside that once stretched between the City of London and Greenwich.

After a 45 minute trip from Westminster Pier to Greenwich, a journey that passes many interesting landmarks, the boat ties up at Greenwich Pier, near the *Cutty Sark,* the late Sir Francis Chichester's *Gypsy Moth IV* and the Royal Naval College. A short walk from the pier brings one to the parish church of Greenwich, St Alphege's, but first a word about Greenwich itself.

Greenwich, a medieval fishing village whose name meant 'green village' to the Saxon and later settlers, owes its rise to fame from the development of its castle area into a palace 'fit for a king and his children'. Built for himself by Humphrey, Duke of Gloucester, by the riverbank, it was called 'Placentia' or 'Bella (beautiful) Court'. It was during the time of the Tudors that it became one of the favourite palaces of the royal family. Henry VIII (1491-1547), Mary I (1516-58) and her half-sister Elizabeth I (1533-1603) were all born here. Having established the shipyards at Deptford and Woolwich, Henry VIII was well able to keep an eye on their progress while out hunting and hawking in Greenwich Park. Armour made at Greenwich was the finest in Europe; there are a number of examples of it in the armouries of the Tower of London.

A raiding party of Danes, in 1012, captured and killed the 28th Archbishop of Canterbury on the site where now stands the parish church of Greenwich, **St Alphege's** (1). The present building, designed by Nicholas Hawksmoor (1661-1736), was built as a result of the collapse of the roof of the previous church, after the parishioners had petitioned Parliament. A committee was set up to consider the application and, at the same time, the situation in regard to other churches in London, Westminster and the suburbs. The result was the passing of the Fifty New Churches Act of 1711, which enabled Greenwich church to be the first of the new churches to be completed.

After damage in the Second World War, the interior of St Alphege's was redesigned by Sir Albert Richardson RA, but the carving by Grinling Gibbons (1648-1721) and the altar rails by Jean Tijou are original. There is also a keyboard, dating from Tudor times, on which Thomas Tallis (*c.*1505-85), 'father of English church music', is said to have played, and here too is the tomb of General James Wolfe, who was born at Westerham in Kent in 1727, died in 1759 at the battle of Quebec in Canada and was buried here.

In Crooms Hill, leading south from the church, is the **Fan Museum** (2), the first of its kind in the world, which opened in 1991.

The late Sir Francis Chichester sailed single-handed around the world in 1967 in **Gipsy Moth IV** (3), named after the aircraft he had flown, and on his return he was knighted by Queen Elizabeth II in front of

St Alphege's parish church, Greenwich, was designed by Hawksmoor.

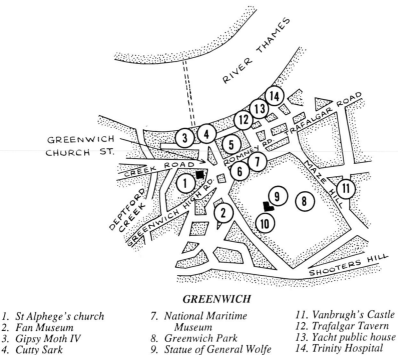

GREENWICH

1. St Alphege's church
2. Fan Museum
3. Gipsy Moth IV
4. Cutty Sark
5. Royal Naval College
6. Queen's House
7. National Maritime Museum
8. Greenwich Park
9. Statue of General Wolfe
10. Flamsteed House and Royal Observatory
11. Vanbrugh's Castle
12. Trafalgar Tavern
13. Yacht public house
14. Trinity Hospital

the Royal Naval College using the sword with which Queen Elizabeth I had knighted Sir Francis Drake.

Walkers wishing to cross the river can do so simply by going under it, using the Greenwich foot tunnel. Built in 1902, it is 370 metres in length, and its northern exit, on the Isle of Dogs, brings one close to the Waterman's Arms. Formerly known as the Newcastle Arms, this pub houses a museum of Victoriana, ranging from stuffed animals to prints of the music hall. The Island Gardens were opened in 1895 and commemorate the place Wren considered to have the best view over the river to Greenwich Palace. The view across the river from Greenwich is now dominated by the sky-scraper at Canary Wharf, part of London's dockland development.

Appropriate to its long connections with the sea, Greenwich was chosen to be the resting place of the last and perhaps the most famous of the old clippers, the **Cutty Sark** (4). She was launched at Dumbarton on the Clyde and registered in London by Captain John Willis, who was familiarly known as 'Old White Hat'. The name *Cutty Sark* was taken from the poem by Robert Burns, 'Tam O' Shanter', in which the witch nannie is described as being lapped and flanged in a cutty sark (a short chemise). The ship was officially opened by Queen Elizabeth on 25th June 1957 and exhibits between decks the story of the *Cutty Sark*,

The entrance to the Fan Museum in Croom's Hill, Greenwich.

as well as the Long John Silver collection of ships' figureheads.

During the reign of William III (1650-1702) and Mary II (1662-94) it was decided to found a hospital for seamen similar to the Royal Hospital for retired soldiers at Chelsea. The site of the King's House was chosen, although at first it was intended to leave this undisturbed, and Christopher Wren (1632-1723) was chosen as architect. Wren was responsible for the general layout of the buildings, but other architects, notably Nicholas Hawksmoor and Sir John Vanbrugh were deeply involved in its construction. Since 1873 the buildings have been used as the **Royal Naval College** (5), a university for serving naval officers, providing them with specialised higher educational training. The principal buildings open to the public include the Painted Hall, the dining hall of the college. The walls and ceiling were painted by Sir James Thornhill (1675-1734) and took him twenty years to complete. He was paid at the rate of £3 per yard for the ceiling and £1 per yard for the walls, with a total bill of £41,000. The ceiling of the lower hall depicts the victory of William and Mary over tyranny and the triumph of the Glorious Revolution. A count revealed that there are 1773$\frac{1}{2}$ bare bosoms on display! The upper hall ceiling shows the Golden Age of Peace and Prosperity under Queen Anne and her husband, Prince George of Denmark.

Across the courtyard from the hall is the chapel of the college; originally designed by Wren, it was rebuilt by James Stuart (1713-88) after a disastrous fire in 1779. The interior design is neo-Grecian and the painting over the east end is by Benjamin West (1738-1820), the American artist, and shows

The Cutty Sark.

The Royal Naval College, Greenwich.

the Preservation of St Paul after his shipwreck on Malta. The quoted fee for the work was £1200, and the cost of the frame by Richard Lawrence was 50 shillings a foot.

The **Queen's House** (6) was originally designed by Inigo Jones in 1616 for Anne of Denmark (1574-1619), the wife of James I. It was not completed until 1635, when Queen Henrietta Maria (1609-69), wife of Charles I, lived in it. At this time the house spanned a main road and from the side gave the impression of being a triumphal arch. Today it is linked by an open colonnade to the National Maritime Museum, of which it forms an integral part. Built in the Palladian style, following the designs of Andrea Palladio (1518-80), the Italian architect, it was the first house in England to break away from the Tudor style of architecture. It has been refurbished by English Heritage.

True to the tradition of royal houses, the Queen's House is said to be haunted.

Under an Act of Parliament of 1934 the **National Maritime Museum** (7) was set up to illustrate the maritime history of Great Britain; it was formally opened by George VI on 27th April 1937. The contents of the museum show the development of Great Britain as a seafaring nation. Among its treasures are the uniform worn by Lord Nelson at the battle of Trafalgar, and the last royal barge, belonging to William and Mary.

In the reign of Henry VI (1421-71), Duke Humphrey fenced in some 80 hectares of what is now **Greenwich Park** (8) and stocked it with deer for royal hunting. Evidence of earlier occupation of the area has been found in the Saxon grave mounds and the remains of a Roman villa. In the early seventeenth century James I replaced the fence with a brick wall, which cost £2000 for its two-mile length. Later in the same century André Le Nôtre (1613-1700), Louis XIV's gardener, laid out the park with avenues of trees. Separating the park from the former gardens of the Queen's House are sunken flowerbeds, which were originally part of the ha-ha (a ditch used as a boundary to avoid the use of walls, fences or hedgerows). Another relic of Tudor days is Queen Elizabeth's oak, round which Elizabeth I's parents, Henry VIII and Anne Boleyn, are said to have danced. Later, according to legend, the tree's hollow stump was used as a lockup for persons who broke the regulations of the park. Many other trees in the grounds are centuries old and are the delight of arboriculturists. The park was first open to the public in the eighteenth century.

On the top of the hill in the park stands the **statue of General Wolfe** (9), by Tait MacKenzie. Wolfe (1727-59) was the conqueror of the Heights of Abraham at Quebec in Canada and lies buried in the parish church of Greenwich.

Flamsteed House (10), named after the first Astronomer Royal, the Reverend Sir John Flamsteed, housed the **Royal Observatory** from 1675 until 1948, when it was moved to Herstmonceux Castle in East Sussex; later it moved again, to Cambridge. It was built on the foundations of the watch-tower of Humphrey, Duke of Gloucester, its cost being defrayed with money obtained from the sale of some old decayed gunpowder. It still stands sentinel over Greenwich from the highest point of the park. It was on this spot in 1428 that the Duke erected a castle which was in use until the building of the observatory. Today the house is an extension of the National Maritime Museum and its exhibition is devoted to astronomy and navigation. In the Octagon Room are several clocks by Thomas Tompion (1639-1713), the father of English clockmaking. In 1965 Prince Philip, the Duke of Edinburgh, inaugurated the Caird Planetarium nearby.

By an international agreement of 1884 in Washington, USA, the meridian of zero longitude runs through Greenwich and is marked by a brass strip on the ground. Like latitude, whose zero line is the Equator, longitude measurements are the means of location from the base line.

Sir John Vanbrugh (1664-1726), soldier, architect and playwright, designed for himself a house on Maze Hill. Known today as **Vanbrugh's Castle** (11), it is modelled on the former Parisian prison, the Bastille, where Sir John was imprisoned between 1690 and 1692 on the charge of spying for the British government. There is a blue plaque on the outside wall of the grounds of the house.

In the past hundred years or so the **Trafalgar Tavern** (12) in Park Road down by the river has served as a place of refreshment, a home for aged seamen, living quarters for members of the Royal Navy, and a men's club. The site was previously occupied by the George Tavern and there is mention of this building in the eleventh century. Charles Dickens (1812-70) mentioned the tavern in *Our Mutual Friend* and here he met for the last time the author Douglas Jerrold (1803-57), whose successful plays included *Black-ey'd Susan* from the ballad by John Gay. The present building was built in 1837 to the designs of Joseph Kay (1775-1847), who was Surveyor to Greenwich Hospital at the time. A pupil of Samuel Pepys Cockerell, Kay became the secretary of the Architects Club and a founder member of the Institute of

British Architects. He was also responsible for the layout of Nelson Street in Greenwich in 1829. Whitebait, once caught in the river nearby, is a speciality of the house and may well have been on the menu at the last Liberal Dinner here to be presided over by William Gladstone in 1883.

In Crane Street, which runs behind the Trafalgar Tavern, is the **Yacht public house** (13), which has stood here for over three hundred years. It has an attractive model yacht sign. Stones engraved with seventeenth-century masons' marks have been found near here, where one can watch the river flow by. The Greenwich meridian line runs through the building.

Continue past the Yacht to **Trinity Hospital** (14), almshouses founded in 1613 by Henry Howard, first Earl of Northampton, for twelve men of Greenwich and eight from Shottisham in Suffolk, the Earl's birthplace. His father, Henry Howard, Earl of Surrey (1517-47), had been executed on a charge of treason and the son found no favour in the court of Elizabeth I; he was arrested in 1571 on the charge of aspiring to marry Mary Stuart. The title lapsed on his death in 1614 and he was buried in the tiny chapel, where his kneeling figure, clad in armour, can still be seen.

The riverside walk leads back to the *Cutty Sark*, passing the grounds of the Royal Naval College, in which one can see the statue of George II and an obelisk to Bellot, a French naval officer who died trying to find the British explorer Franklin, lost in northern Canada.

The Trinity Hospital almshouses, Greenwich.

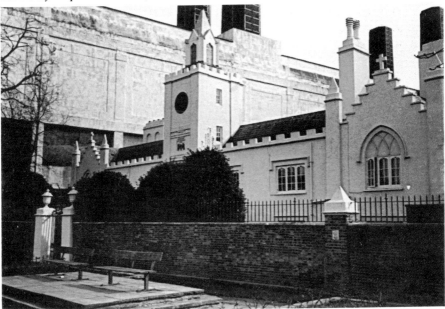

Hammersmith Pier.

Chiswick Mall.

9
Hammersmith

Originally built in 1864 slightly to the north of its present position, the Metropolitan Line **underground station** (1) was rebuilt four years later on the present site. From the corner of the road here it is possible to see the District and Piccadilly Lines station; it was first constructed in 1874 but had to be rebuilt after a fire in 1882. Note the titles of the railway companies which formerly operated their services here.

Hammersmith is first mentioned in the thirteenth century and the name is said to derive from either a 'home', or town, with a hithe — a small dock built into the bank of the river — or from a smithy, with the 'hammer' and 'smythe' joining to become the town's own name. In its present spelling the name is recorded in a document of 1675.

Using the subway, cross to the opposite side of the road. On the corner of Hammersmith Broadway and Hammersmith Road stands the **Convent of the Sacred Heart** (2) designed by John Bentley, the architect of Westminster Cathedral. It dates from 1876 and houses, as well as the nuns, two schools for Roman Catholic children.

Turn away from the convent to the Butterwick, now the local bus station; its name comes from the manor house which stood round the corner opposite the church. Continuing through the bus station, the road leads towards the Hammersmith Flyover and round two corners to the former garden front of the manor house of the **Butterwick** (3).

To cross the road safely find the subway by the underground station, and take the left-hand exit up to **St Paul's church** (4). The present building was erected in 1882 to the designs of Roumieu, Gough and Seddon but it contains several items from previous centuries. The font dates from the seventeenth century, as do the chairs in the chancel, while the pulpit, designed by Sir Christopher Wren, came from the church of All Hallows, Thames Street, in the City of London. Monuments worth noting include one to Sir Nicholas Crisp, a Royalist at the time of the Civil War. He helped Charles I raise an army and had inscribed on his monument, erected during his lifetime, the words 'that glorious martyr King Charles the First of blessed memory'. There is also a monument to Sir Samuel Morland, the inventor of a water pump for use in Windsor Castle.

Leave the churchyard by the south-east corner and the flyover is immediately overhead. Pass underneath and a National **Car Park** (5) is on the right. By crossing through the car park Hammersmith Bridge Road is reached.

Opposite is a public house, the **Oxford and Cambridge** (6), appropriately situated by the road that leads to the river and one of the best vantage points for watching the Boat Race.

To the side of the roadway are the **Digby Mansions** (7); on the side of the approach wall to the bridge an old public drinking fountain can be seen, though no longer in working order.

It is not far from the fountain to the riverbank, from where we can take a look at

Drinking fountain on the wall near Hammersmith Bridge.

Hammersmith Bridge (8). Designed by Sir Joseph Bazalgette, who also engineered the Thames embankments, it was built in 1884-7 and replaced the earlier bridge, built in 1827 by Tierney Clark, which was the first suspension bridge over the Thames. The later bridge uses the piers of its predecessor to support its towers. On the wooden handrail on the upstream side of the bridge is a small metal plaque recording the gallant deed of Charles Wood, an officer in the Royal Air Force, who saved a drowning woman by diving from the bridge. The coats of arms on the bridge are the arms of Guildford, Kent, Middlesex and the former Metropolitan Board of Works.

The riverside walk here is called the **Lower Mall** (9) and leads from the bridge past Hammersmith Pier to the Dove public house. Almost immediately you will come to a short row of eighteenth-century houses. Number 6 is the headquarters of the Amateur Rowing Association and number 10 is a fine example of the style of Robert Adam, though not actually designed by him. Note the very fine doorway and the wrought-iron railings and gate. Among the riverside taverns here are the Blue Anchor and the Rutland, which displays that family's coat of arms.

The **Furnivall Gardens** (10), whose name commemorates one of the borough's great benefactors, occupy the site that until 1936 was Hammersmith Creek. A few metres back from the river stands **Westcott Lodge** (11); it was once the vicarage. The old-fashioned lamp holder on the side of the house once lit a street in West Berlin; it was presented to the borough by Willy Brandt, the Mayor of West Berlin, as a symbol of the friendship between the two places.

Hammersmith Pier (12), which also dates from the filling in of the old creek, is widely used during the summer by the boats that take visitors on trips up and down the Thames. Across the gardens can be seen Hammersmith Town Hall; its rebuilding started in the late 1930s but the modern extensions, on the King Street side, were opened in 1970. On the other side of the river can be seen the new St Paul's School. The school was founded in the sixteenth century by Dean Colet for 153 poor boys. At first it was housed in the churchyard of St Paul's Cathedral but it occupied a site in Hammersmith Road from 1885 until it moved to its present site.

It is a short walk to the other half of Hammersmith's Mall, the Upper Mall, and a step back into the atmosphere of the seventeenth and eighteenth centuries. Number 15 has two inscriptions on it recording that the **Doves Bindery** (13) and private printing press were here and that Thomas Sanderson lived here.

The **Dove public house** (14), dating from the seventeenth century, has much to offer the passer-by both in history and in refresh-

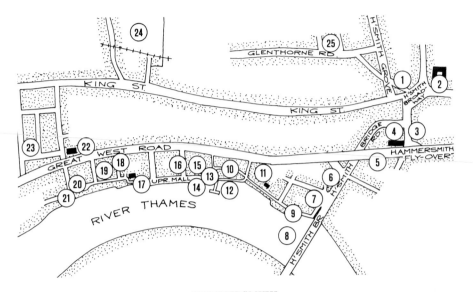

HAMMERSMITH

1. Underground station
2. Convent of the Sacred Heart
3. Butterwick manor house
4. St Paul's church
5. Car park
6. Oxford and Cambridge
7. Digby Mansions
8. Hammersmith Bridge
9. Lower Mall
10. Furnivall Gardens
11. Westcott Lodge
12. Hammersmith Pier
13. Doves Bindery
14. Dove public house
15. Kelmscott House
16. Rivercourt Road
17. Linden House
18. Oil Mill Lane
19. Hammersmith pumping station
20. Black Lion
21. Hammersmith Terrace
22. St Peter's church
23. St Peter's Square
24. Ravenscourt Park
25. St John's church

ment. The pub is mentioned in a number of literary works.

Next along the Mall is **Kelmscott House** (15), dating from the 1780s. William Morris lived here from 1878 to 1896, using the stables for holding meetings. He set up a tapestry loom in one of the bedrooms and the Kelmscott Press in the cottage of number 14. Some of the rooms in the house are still decorated with wallpaper designed by Morris. Plaques recall Morris and George Macdonald, the poet and novelist who also lived here.

Rivercourt Road (16), leading down to the river, is a reminder of the court that ruled over the river in days long ago.

Continuing along the Upper Mall past the eighteenth-century house used by Latymer School, we come to **Linden House** (17), a Queen Anne style house and the home of the London Corinthian Sailing Club. Just beyond the house is a short arcade under the modern houses built slightly nearer the river than the other buildings we have already seen.

Turn away from the river to the side of Linden House and the path takes the explorer to the busy Great West Road, passing a collection of houses of the nineteenth and twentieth centuries in **Oil Mill Lane** (18).

At the junction of this quiet backwater

William Morris's press room at Kelmscott House, Hammersmith, during the printing of the Kelmscott Chaucer.

and the busy dual carriageway turn left and shortly the waterworks appear. Belonging to the Thames Water Authority, the **Hammersmith pumping station** (19) delivers 45 million gallons (200 million litres) of water each day to the West End and west London. The building dates from 1811 and was designed by W. Tierney Clark, architect of the previous Hammersmith Bridge. The building incorporates a seventeenth-century structure which may have been a riverside gatehouse for one of the great houses that stood here then. It is just possible that the gate was the one that led to the house of Charles II's widow, Catharine of Braganza, whose gardens were mentioned by John Evelyn in his diary.

Passing the waterworks on the left, con-tinue to walk along the pavement of the Great West Road to South Black Lion Lane. At the end of the lane is the **Black Lion** public house (20), a pleasant nineteenth-century house.

Looking through the open space on the left we can see the modern riverside houses mentioned when considering Linden House. But at this junction can be found **Hammersmith Terrace** (21), a set of sixteen identical houses whose front doors open straight on to the pavement, while their backs look directly on to the river. The noted Royal Academician Philip de Loutherbourg lived in numbers 7 and 8 in the late eighteenth century; while here he was 'taken to prophecy and healing', an activity which greatly amused Walpole, who made him a subject of a number of his letters. A later resident of number 7 was Sir Emery Walker, the typographer and friend of William Morris. He and Morris together founded the Kelmscott Press. His house is now marked with a blue plaque.

Shortly after Sir Emery's house the Hammersmith Upper Mall joins with the Chiswick Mall and we must leave the riverside walk and, turning right, follow the course of the road, Eyot Gardens, back to the Great West Road. Here turn right, back towards the centre of Hammersmith, passing Verbena Gardens, and walking to the subway under the Great West Road. Use the subway to reach **St Peter's church** (22). The church was built between 1827 and 1829 and is the oldest church in Hammersmith. Its architect, Edward Lapidge, was an assistant to the famous landscape designer Lancelot 'Capability' Brown and later became the County Surveyor for Surrey. The church is built of yellow brick and its chief glory is the Ionic porch at the west end. Many of the fittings are original and have been well preserved.

St Peter's Square (23) was described by one architectural historian as being like a suburban Belgravia. Built between 1825 and 1830, it does give an impression of that fashionable district, though on a smaller scale.

Leave the square by way of St Peter's Villas, which road joins Black Lion Lane. By turning left into the lane King Street is reached. This is the busy high street of Hammersmith and there is much to see, but we shall make a pleasant diversion into **Ravenscourt Park** (24). The manor of Pallenswick was granted to Alice Perrers, the mistress of Edward III, in 1373, but after her banishment five years later the property was seized by the crown. In 1813 a document refers to the ownership of the house by George Scott and describes it as being the 'manor house lately called Ravenscourt'. The public park covering 14 hectares was opened in 1888, with pleasant paths, lawns and an old English garden.

Return to King Street and walk along to Studland Road. Turn left and soon, after passing under the District and Piccadilly Lines railway bridge, turn right into Glenthorne Road. The continual growth of population in the nineteenth century made it necessary to build many new churches to accommodate all the people. One of the newer churches of Hammersmith is **St John's church** (25), which was built in 1859 to the designs of William Butterfield.

It is a short walk from here to Beadon Road, which leads back to Hammersmith Broadway and the Metropolitan Line station.

Left: *Fenton House, Hampstead.*

Below: *The Keats House museum, Hampstead.*

10
Hampstead

Hampstead underground station (1) is the deepest in London's system, being 63 metres below the surface. Using the Northern Line of the Underground railway it is possible today to leave the City of London and arrive at Hampstead in half an hour, but less than a century ago the journey would have been far more arduous.

First mentioned in a charter of King Edgar in 957, the manor of Hampstead is recorded in 986 as having been given by Ethelred to Westminster Abbey, which owned it until 1550 and the dissolution of the abbey. By the seventeenth century there were a few houses, and merchants from the City moved their families here to flee from plague-ridden London, commuting each day by horse or coach. In a gazetteer published in 1880 Hampstead is given as being four miles from London.

Church Row (2) has been described by many authorities as the best street in Hampstead. A variety of houses of the eighteenth century are to be seen here, and on one of them is a plaque commemorating John James Park (1795-1833), the author of a history of Hampstead.

In the churchyard of the parish church, **St John's** (3), can be found many famous names engraved on the tombstones. Explorers who know that the main entrance to a church is the west door and that the altars, or holy tables, are always at the east, should be warned that this church is not correctly orientated — look up at the weathervane and you will see! Tucked away in the southeast corner of the churchyard lie John Con-

stable (1776-1837), the artist, his wife and some of their children. A few yards south of the church wall can be seen the grave of John Harrison (1693-1776), the inventor of the chronometer. Across the road — Church Row — is the extension to the churchyard. Here, near to the railings, are the graves of Hugh Gaitskell (1903-63), Leader of the Labour Party from 1955; Kay Kendall (Harrison), actress; Anton Walbrook, actor; and George Du Maurier (1834-96), the illustrator and novelist.

In 1816 the Abbé Morel, with a group of French refugees, settled in Hampstead and built a church, which they dedicated to St Mary. Today the interior of **St Mary's** (4) comes as a pleasant surprise to the explorer of Hampstead. The statue of the Blessed Virgin Mary is a model of the statue that overlooks Buenos Aires, the capital of Argentina. The founder's tomb is just inside the door, covered by a mat.

Halfway up a flight of steps which lead from Heath Street to Holly Mount is **Golden Yard** (5). Dating from the seventeenth century, the delightful houses in this little courtyard make the diversion from the main road well worthwhile.

A charming little cul-de-sac, **Holly Mount** (6) once possessed a chapel, now number 17, in which John Wesley is believed to have preached.

Turn right at the top of Holly Bush Hill and you will find the **Holly Bush public house** (7). Built in 1643, its sign reminds one of the custom of hanging a green branch or bush, by way of advertisement, outside a

The chalybeate well in Well Walk, Hampstead.

house licensed to sell ale. Once connected with the house next door, Romney's House, when it was used as the Constitutional Club, today it provides a quiet haven away from the traffic. Visitors to the tavern have included Marie Lloyd, 'Two-ton' Tessie O'Shea, Dr Samuel Johnson and James Boswell, Oliver Goldsmith, Leigh Hunt and Charles Lamb.

Romney's House (8) was bought by George Romney, the famous portrait artist, in 1796 for £700, with rates of £50 per year. The house had been built originally at the turn of the eighteenth century and was complete with stables when Romney moved in. His first task was to have the stables removed for, although he was fond of horse-riding, he did not like riding in public, and he had an indoor studio built instead, with a

gallery and living room attached. A side entrance led to the gallery, where he entertained his mistresses. After Romney left the house and resold it, the brewer at the Holly Bush bought it and turned it into the Hampstead Constitutional Club, linking it, by a specially made door, to the tavern round the corner. Later the house was divided into two as a private house — and so it remains.

Across the green formed by the junction of Holly Bush Hill, Frognal Rise and Hampstead Grove stands **Bolton House** (9), with its commemorative plaque announcing that Joanna Brillie (1762-1851), the Scottish poetess and dramatist, lived in the house. Walter Scott was a frequent visitor here and once wrote that he looked forward to visiting it. Joanna's tragedies are described as the best written by any woman of the period. John Kemble, the actor-manager, and his sister Sarah Siddons acted in some of her plays.

Fenton House (10) is an excellent example of a late seventeenth-century Hampstead house, the date 1693 being painted on a plaque over the entrance. The identity of the architect is unknown, but Sir Christopher Wren has been suggested; neither is it known who the original owner was. In the early eighteenth century it is listed as Ostend House but by 1786 it had become known as Clock House. A certain P. I. Fenton bought the house in 1793 and it has been known as Fenton House ever since. It is now owned by the National Trust and is the home of the Benton Fletcher Collection of keyboard instruments and the Benning Collection of porcelain and furniture. The latter collection was part of the estate given to the Trust with the house in 1936 by the late Lady Benning, the owner. A painting in the Morning Room, by John Constable, shows Hampstead Heath in the eighteenth century.

HAMPSTEAD
1. Hampstead under-
   ground station
2. Church Row
3. St John's church and
   churchyard
4. St Mary's Catholic
   church
5. Golden Yard
6. Holly Mount
7. Holly Bush public
   house
8. Romney's House
9. Bolton House
10. Fenton House
11. Old and New Grove
    Houses
12. Admiral's House
13. Whitestone Pond
14. Vale of Health and
    Keats House
15. Jack Straw's Castle
16. Hampstead Heath
17. Leg of Mutton Pond
18. Spaniards Inn

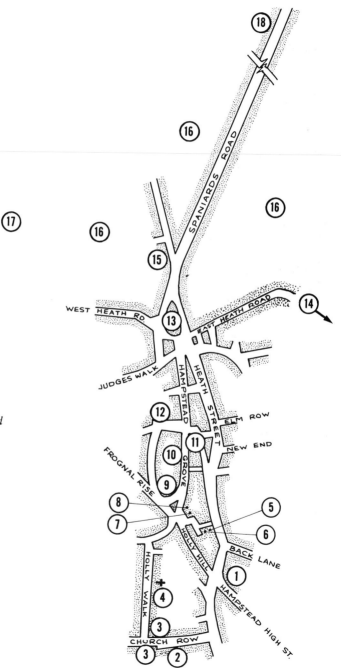

THIS PLUM TREE
REPLACES THE ONE BENEATH WHICH
JOHN KEATS WROTE
ODE TO A NIGHTINGALE

In the spring of 1819 a nightingale had built her nest near my house. Keats felt a tranquil and continual joy in her song and one morning he took his chair from the breakfast table to the grass-plot under a plum tree, where he sat for two or three hours. When he came into the house, I perceived he had some scraps of paper in his hand, and these he was quietly thrusting behind the books.

CHARLES ARMITAGE BROWN *to* LORD HOUGHTON

The plaque at Keats House, Hampstead, marking the spot where John Keats wrote 'Ode to a Nightingale'.

Belonging to the eighteenth century are **Old and New Grove Houses** (11). In the latter lived the architect Henry Flitcroft (1679-1769), while in the former, as a brown plaque on the wall records, lived the Du Maurier family.

George IV had an admiral by the name of Barton who, when he retired from the sea, came to live in Hampstead, in what is **Admiral's House** (12) today. He converted the roof into a quarterdeck of a ship and, on 'high feasts and holydays' raised the White Ensign and fired his cannon in celebration. Constable painted the house in his picture 'The Romantic House of Hampstead', which is in the Tate Gallery in London. A plaque on the wall tells of George Gilbert Scott, the architect (1811-78), and his family living here in the nineteenth century, but they found it too cold in the winter and moved back into London. In the cottage to the side

of the house lived John Galsworthy (1867-1933), the author of *The Forsyte Saga*.

Mr Pickwick delivered a lecture to the members of the Pickwick Club on the subject of the source of the Hampstead Ponds. The flagpole at **Whitestone Pond** (13) marks the highest spot in the London area — 144 metres above sea-level. Opposite the pond is the village pound, where stray animals were kept until redeemed by their owners. There is an inscription on a stone which reads ANNO 1787.

East Heath Road leads to Keats Grove through the **Vale of Health** (14) which is one of a number of small hamlets round about Hampstead Heath. Leigh Hunt (1784-1859) came in 1816 to live here and extols its beauty in his poems. He lived in one of the earliest cottages in the Vale which, alas, has long since been pulled down to make way for less suitable buildings. It was after having stayed with Hunt that Keats, too, took a great liking to Hampstead and became a resident in Wentworth Place from 1817 to 1820. His house, the **Keats House** museum, was built in 1815-16 and completely restored in 1974-5.

A favourite walk of Charles Dickens, we are told, was across Hampstead Heath to a meal at **Jack Straw's Castle** (15) — not that he saw the present building, as it was rebuilt after the Second World War. Whether the name comes from Jack Straw, a ringleader in the Peasants' Revolt of 1381, or from a Jane Straw who once lived here, is still being debated in all its bars. Other recorded visitors include William Thackeray, Robert Louis Stevenson, Wilkie Collins and John Forster, biographer of Dickens. In the eighteenth century horse-races took place behind the inn but attracted undesirable elements and were closed down in the same century. It was also the meeting place of the Court Leet of the manor of Hampstead.

Hampstead Heath (16) is one of the few remaining wild pieces of open space in the London area — others include Wimbledon Common and Epping Forest. Today it comprises over 320 hectares but the original public purchase in 1871 was East, West and Sandy Heaths. Gradually over the next hundred years other land was acquired. Except at bank holiday fair time, the heath offers peace and quiet with miles of paths for pleasant walks. Like other open spaces, the Heath has memories of highwaymen. Tales are told of Dick Turpin and his famous ride to York and of Jackson who in 1673 was hanged for highway murder behind Jack Straw's Castle.

Leg of Mutton Pond (17) was dug before 1825 by unemployed poor of the parish.

Originally built in the seventeenth century, the **Spaniards Inn** (18) was at the entrance to the Bishop of London's park. The tollhouse opposite is now scheduled as an ancient monument. The inn has strong literary and historical connections. The fictional account of Dick Turpin's ride to York mentions the Spaniards, and there is a display of keys and pistols said to have belonged to the highwayman, together with leg-irons used to secure him in Newgate prison. Dickens uses the place as the scene of a tea-party for Mrs Bardell in *Pickwick Papers* and of the arrest in her breach of promise case against Pickwick. At the time of the Gordon Riots (1780-1), the inn's landlord, Giles Thomas, detained the rioters who were on their way to wreck Kenwood, the home of Lord Mansfield. He succeeded in diverting their attention long enough to allow an ostler to rouse a party of the Horse Guards, who detained them.

How the tavern acquired its name is open to conjecture, but there are two possible suggestions: that the house was once occupied by members of the Spanish embassy staff and so became known as the Spaniards' House; alternatively that the tavern was owned by two Spanish brothers in the eighteenth century, but they both fell in love with the same woman and fought a duel in the yard of the inn. When the winner entered the house the woman had disappeared. He then returned to the yard and buried his brother there.

Highgate Cemetery.

Lauderdale House, Highgate.

11
Highgate

With its spire pointing towards the sky, St Michael's church, Highgate, stands on London's northern heights. Seen from a distance, it reminds one of the existence of a tiny village now completely absorbed by the metropolis.

Riding along on the crest of the hill, Highgate is 139 metres above the river Thames, and, looking out over towards the City of London, one is standing above the level of the cross on the top of St Paul's Cathedral. Although Hampstead Heath is over 6 metres higher than the village, it does not appear so when wandering on it. Perhaps it is the steepness of the descents on three sides, the north face being the only one which remains fairly level for some distance, that gives the impression of a greater height here at Highgate.

Opposite the church, at **number 3 The Grove** (1), lived Samuel Taylor Coleridge (1772-1834), the poet and literary critic, born in the vicarage of Ottery St Mary, Devon. He was educated at Christ's Hospital, London (a plaque in Newgate Street in the City marks the spot where the school was founded) and later studied at Jesus College, Cambridge. He spent the last eighteen years of his life living with James Gillman in Highgate and on his death in July 1834 was buried in the burial ground of the old school chapel. The Gillmans erected a memorial to him in the church, the first to be placed in the new building, and in 1961 his body, together with those of his daughter, Sara, and her husband, were reinterred in the church. The first six houses of The

Grove were erected between 1682 and 1685 but the Gillmans' house is the least altered of the set of semi-detached houses, which appear to have been built to a single specification.

At the end of the sixteenth century, John Norden in his *Speculum Britanniae* wrote: 'upon this hill is a most pleasant dwelling.' He was referring to Dorchester House, in the garden of which now stand the houses of The Grove. The home of Henry, Lord Marquess of Dorchester, the house was to have been a charity school for girls under a plan set up by the son of a local resident, William Blake, who was described by Lysons in his *Environs of London*, published in 1791, as being 'a crazy philanthropist, a woollen draper at the sign of the Golden Boy in Maiden Lane, Covent Garden'. The children were to be 'decently cloathed in blew, lined with yellow; constantly fed all alike with good wholsom diet, taught to read, write, and cast accompts (accounts), and so put out to trades, in order to live another day'. Unfortunately Blake did not receive the financial support that he had hoped for, and the school came to an abrupt end in 1685, by which time the houses of The Grove had been built.

It seems that Highgate Grove or Green was the recognised place for all the local revelries and fairs to take place up to the eighteenth century. Here in July 1744, at the time of the Highgate Fair, a sack race was organised when the landlord gave a pair of gloves as a prize. A pig was to be turned loose on the Wednesday of the fair and 'who ever catches it by the tail, throws it over his head, shall have it'. Surrounded by elms of great beauty and age, the green must have presented an attractive sight then. Before leaving The Grove look back and admire Widanhurst, built in the style of William and Mary, with a west wing dating from the early eighteenth century.

The provision of drinking water has always been a problem of supply and demand and the presence of an **underground reservoir** here (2) reminds one of the need today. This portion of South Grove contains a number of houses of the eighteenth and nineteenth centuries which are worth noting.

Lysons says that the setting up of a 'gate upon the hill' gives the village its name. Today the **Gatehouse Tavern** (3), standing on the borders of the former parishes of Hornsey and St Pancras, has little to commend it architecturally, but its name refers to the fact that here, in the middle ages, stood one of the three gatehouse entrances to the 'Greate Park of Haringhey, alias Hornsey', belonging to the Bishops of London. The other two entrances were at the Spaniards, Hampstead, and at Newgate, near East Finchley railway station; nothing remains today of either.

Nearby, too, was the 'high-gate', the first tollgate to be erected in England, and which was guarded by the hermit of Highgate. This same man constructed the pond and, when his own private resources ceased, was ordered by the king, Edward III (1312-77), to set up the bar across the road here; the tolls from this helped to pay for the building of the road of the 'hollow-way'.

There are a number of inns in the area, including the Gatehouse, which are connected with the old custom of 'swearing on the horns'. This ancient practice takes place twice a year, when, for a small fee donated to a local charity, anyone can become a 'freeman' of Highgate.

Before the London Government Act of 1963 the Gatehouse Tavern lay half in Hornsey, then in the former county of Middlesex, and half in the borough of St Pancras. In previous times the Middlesex Sessions were held in an old courtroom on the second floor, and the London side of the room was roped off to make sure that the prisoners did not escape to another authority's area.

In 1565 Sir Robert Cholmeley founded the 'Free Grammar School of Sir Roger Cholmeley', the chapel of which stood on the site of the former hermitage of St Michael. Old Highgate was never a parish in its own right but the chapel developed into being a chapel of ease, that is a place for public worship for the use of parishioners living a distance from the parish church, for the parishes of both Hornsey and St Pancras, as well as being the school chapel. However, in 1826 a judgement in the Court of Chancery, one of the three divisions of the High Court of Justice, ruled that the public had no right to be there, and with the re-endowment of the school its chapel reverted to private use. The school buildings were rebuilt in 1819 and the statutes remodelled in 1824. Today **Highgate School** (4) is a flourishing one with several hundred boys on its roll. A number of old monuments from the school chapel have been re-erected in St Michael's parish church. The old chapel of the school was demolished in 1833, when the present one in the early French Gothic style took its place, while in the 1860s further rebuilding of the school premises replaced older structures, but the old burial ground on the corner of Southwood Lane remains as a reminder of its past association with the parish.

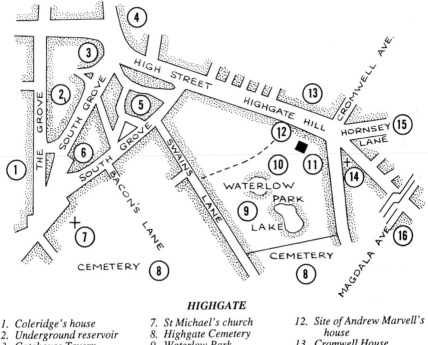

HIGHGATE

1. Coleridge's house	7. St Michael's church	12. Site of Andrew Marvell's
2. Underground reservoir	8. Highgate Cemetery	house
3. Gatehouse Tavern	9. Waterlow Park	13. Cromwell House
4. Highgate School	10. Statue of Sir Sydney	14. St Joseph's Catholic church
5. Pond Square	Waterlow	15. Archway
6. The Flask tavern	11. Lauderdale House	16. Whittington's Stone

Southwood Lane, picturesque and winding, contains Southwood House, dating from 1746 with a porch added later in the same century. Also in the lane are the Woolaston-Paunceforth Almshouses, rebuilt in the 1720s.

A short walk down the High Street, with its many interesting shops and houses, is South Grove, in which there are several fine buildings. It was while staying at Arundel House, whose site is now occupied by Old Hall, that Francis Bacon (1561-1626), philosopher and writer (and a contender for the privilege of having written Shakespeare's plays), died. His death was caused, according to tradition, through a chill he had caught while experimenting with a primitive form of refrigeration by stuffing a fowl with snow.

Forming part of the original, much larger village green is **Pond Square** (5); its Georgian cottages were an early encroachment on an area dedicated to entertainment in medieval days. The pond itself has long since disappeared and asphalt has taken the place of water. In his book *Worthies of England* Dr Thomas Fuller (1608-61) compliments the hermit of Highgate for excavating Highgate Pond, so providing a hollow at the top of the hill to catch water, and for using the gravel out of the pit to construct a causeway in the hollow-way (Holloway Road) to take travellers safely on their way to the City of London. It is said that the square is haunted by the chicken which was stuffed with snow by Francis Bacon.

No village scene is complete without its pub and Highgate's is called **The Flask** (6). Although opinions vary as to the exact date of the first tavern on this site, all agree that the present building is late seventeenth-century. The inn was the meeting place in the eighteenth century of a number of distinguished artists, amongst whom was William Hogarth (1697-1764), who witnessed the quarrel between two drinkers that resulted in one felling the other by striking him with a pint pot. The look on the stricken man's face turned from anguish to a hideous grin, and Hogarth quickly sketched the scene to the amusement of both men. There are also a number of stories told that link Dick Turpin with the Flask and tell how, on one occasion, he jumped the nearby high-gate with Black Bess when being pursued — or did he merely hide in the cellars? The Flask is also linked with the custom of swearing on the horns. Some authorities claim that the practice originated here with drovers bringing their cattle from the Midlands to Smithfield. They formed themselves into a fraternity, entry to which required the applicant to take an oath and kiss the horns — perhaps originally on the ox itself. The name 'The Flask' recalls that water from the nearby Hampstead Wells was sold here in the eighteenth century, in flasks. Another visitor in the eighteenth century was Major Robert Rogers, who discovered the land route to the North-west Passage of North America. Rogers's Rangers have a place in the history of America as a band of frontiersmen who fought with British troops during the French-Indian war between 1756 and 1763. In the American War of Independence (1775-6) there was a justifiable doubt as to where Rogers's loyalties lay and both sides rejected his services. On his return to Britain he settled in London, where he died in 1795.

The parish church of Highgate, **St Michael's** (7), was designed by Lewis Vulliamy (1791-1871) in 1830, with a chancel added by George Edmund Street (1824-81) in the year of his death. Vulliamy, the son of Benjamin Vulliamy the clockmaker, designed several London churches, including the now demolished Christ Church, Woburn Square, but is best known for Dorchester House in Park Lane, which was demolished in 1929 to make way for the Dorchester Hotel. The cost of the church was borne equally by the Church Commissioners and the parishioners and

The tomb of George Eliot in Highgate Cemetery.

amounted to £10,000. On the site stood Ashurst House, shown on early maps as the Mansion House and built for Sir William Ashurst, Lord Mayor of London in 1694. The house was demolished in 1830 to make way for the church.

On the southern slopes of the hill, to the east of St Michael's, lies **Highgate Cemetery** (8), now accessible only from Swains Lane. The cemetery was laid out in 1838 by David Ramsay, who was the London Cemetery Company's landscape gardener. Incorporated by an Act of Parliament, the company's task was to establish private cemeteries in the northern, eastern and southern suburbs of London. The entrance to the older portion of the cemetery, in Swains Lane, was the work of Stephen Geary (c.1797-1854), who specialised in laying out cemeteries, 'an architect whose taste and ability have been long and justly appreciated'. Directly below St Michael's church are the catacombs, with their Egyptian-style portal and vaults dug into the side of the hill; through the open doors of some may be seen the coffins resting on their shelves. This portion of the cemetery is dominated by the mausoleum of Julius Beer, with a stepped pyramid at its top, in the form of the mausoleum of Halicarnassus, and designed by John Oldrid Scott (1841-1913), the second son of Sir George Gilbert Scott, with interior sculpture by Henry Armstead. The cemetery today, with its extension of 1854, contains 51,000 graves. Most notable is that of Karl Marx (1818-83), whose book *Das Kapital*, the first volume of which was published in 1867, was used by Lenin as a basis for the teaching and development of communism, and which led to the formation of the Union of Soviet Socialist Republics in 1917. Here too are the parents of Charles Dickens; George Eliot (1819-80),

whose real name was Mary Ann Evans and who was the author of *Adam Bede, The Mill on the Floss* and *Felix Holt*; Tom Sayers (1825-65), a famous prizefighter; Michael Faraday (1791-1867), the British chemist and physicist whose work in the field of electricity developed the magneto and the dynamo; and John Frederick Dennison Maurice (1805-72), founder of the Working Man's College at Camden Town. The inscription on another memorial reads: 'William Friese-Greene, inventor of kinematography. His genius bestowed upon humanity the boon of commercial kinematography, of which he was the first inventor and patentee.' Friese-Greene (1865-1921) first showed moving pictures in public in 1890, at number 20 Brooke Street, Holborn.

Sir Sydney Waterlow gave 10 hectares of land to Londoners in 1889, and two years later **Waterlow Park** (9) was open to the public. The park has many attractions, including two ponds with a wide variety of waterfowl, an aviary, quiet gardens and, during the summer months, a grass theatre where drama, opera and ballet are performed.

The **Statue of Sir Sydney Waterlow** (10), Lord Mayor of London 1872-3, was erected in his memory with money collected, mainly from the poor of the district, in 1900. Collecting boxes in the park realised as much as £18 in one day, and all in coins of less than one shilling. In Sir Sydney's right hand are an umbrella and trilby hat.

Standing within the grounds of Waterlow Park is **Lauderdale House** (11), dating from the sixteenth century, with additions in the seventeenth and eighteenth centuries. It belonged to the second Earl (later Duke) of Lauderdale (1616-82). While the Earl

Left: *Cromwell House, Highgate.*

Right: *The Archway, Highgate.*

was in Scotland, Charles II installed Nell Gwynne in the house, and it is said that on one occasion when the king was passing by Nell held a child out of an upstairs window by a leg and called to Charles: 'Name this child.' To this the king replied: 'God save the Earl of Burford.' It should be added that this story is repeated elsewhere in the kingdom but the earldom changes with the place! Samuel Pepys (1633-1703), the diarist, records a visit to the house in July 1666, when he listened to one of the servants playing a violin and to Lord Lauderdale reflecting on his hatred of music, particularly the lute and bagpipe.

Leaving Lauderdale House by its front gates, turn left and walk a short way up Highgate High Street to a **plaque** (12) mark- ing the site of the cottage in which lived Andrew Marvell (1621-78), the poet and assistant to John Milton in the Latin secretaryship to the Council, and later member of Parliament for Hull.

On the opposite side of the roadway to the Marvell plaque is the misnamed **Cromwell House** (13); although the house is contemporary with the Lord Protector, having been built in 1630, there is no direct evidence that he ever lived in it at any time of his life. Perhaps it was the carved newel posts of the staircase that gave rise to the suggestion that General Ireton, son-in-law to Oliver Cromwell, lived in the house. However, according to the London Survey Committee researching the house and its history, both these suggestions are baseless. John

Ireton, the general's brother, obtained possession of Lauderdale House in 1651 and lived there until the Restoration of the monarchy in 1660, when the Earl of Lauderdale's property was restored to him.

In reply to the Anglican domination of the skyline with St Michael's church, the Roman Catholic church of **St Joseph** (14) matches well from the other side of Waterlow Park and can be seen from a comparable distance. The church was built in 1875-6 in the Italianate style by Tasker.

Highgate Hill has always proved a formidable proposition for heavy traffic, in spite of the fact that the road was on gravel and would therefore stay firm even in the wettest of conditions. However, early in the nineteenth century plans were made for an alternative road to be constructed with a lesser incline. After an abortive attempt to build a tunnel through the hill, a deep cutting was made on the recommendation of Sir John Rennie (1794-1874), the second son of John Rennie, the bridge-builder and civil engineer. This new road cut off two portions of Hornsey Lane, and John Nash (1752-1835) designed the first **Archway** (15) over the new road. Its steel successor, designed by Sir Alexander Binnie, Chief Engineer of the London County Council, in 1897 affords an excellent view from these northern heights across the sprawling metropolis and towards the City of London.

Returning from Archway to St Joseph's church, the walker will find himself at the top of Highgate Hill. With the view of London before him, he can well imagine the bells of the City pealing out their messages of welcome over the past hundreds of years. Standing on the roadside on Highgate Hill is the stone known as **Whittington's Stone** (16). It is said to have been here when young Richard Whittington (*c*.1358-1423), later four times Lord Mayor of London, feeling despondent, left London to return to Gloucester. Quite how he planned to do this is a puzzle to many people because he was on the wrong road for Gloucester. However, the story-books and the pantomimes tell us that he rested here, where he heard the bells of St Mary-le-Bow, in Cheapside, ring out a 'message' for him: 'Turn again Whittington, thrice Lord Mayor of London.' He did return to the City and fulfilled the prophecy. The present stone dates from 1821 and replaces the original one, which is believed to have been the base of a wayside cross and which had been removed in the eighteenth century and placed at the end of Queen's Head Lane.

In the reign of Edward IV, William Poole fell ill with leprosy and founded a hospital, a lazar-house, near where the Whittington Stone is today on Highgate Hill. The wayside cross referred to was outside the hospital. In his will Richard Cloudesley left 6s 8d 'to the poor lazars of Hyegate', to pray for him by name in their bede-roll.

12
Islington

Before the coming of the Romans this area was covered by the great forest of Middlesex but later developed as 'the hill or down of Gisla', as shown in the Anglo-Saxon Chronicle, into a village around the Upper and Lower Roads. Today these streets, the latter renamed Essex Road, meet at Islington Green.

Starting at Angel underground station, it is a short walk to the **Angel** (1), once a famous coaching inn and later an equally famous Lyons Corner House teashop, and now a bank. Here we turn right into the High Street which leads us towards Upper and Lower Streets. Weekday walkers will find much to distract them from exploring the former village, for there are shops and an open-air market as well as Camden Passage antique centre just beyond the Green.

By the Green, in the former **Royal Agricultural Hall** (2), built in 1862 by the Smithfield Club for an annual cattle show, is the Business Design Centre.

Crossing the road to the edge of what remains of the old village green, we find the **statue of Sir Hugh Myddleton** (3), a sixteenth-century Welshman who founded a company that brought fresh spring water from Amwell, near Ware in Hertfordshire, to the City of London. The sculptor was John Thomas.

Islington Green (4) lies at the junction of Upper Street and Essex Road and was given to the parish by the lord of the manor. For many years it was a piece of unenclosed waste land used by the parishioners as a rubbish dump, but it was enclosed in 1777.

In the centre stood the cage or prison and a pair of stocks. The green was also used as a place of assembly and after the passing of the Reform Act in 1832 the hustings and polling booth for the area were set up here.

On the far side of the Green was the famous **Collins music hall** (5), marked by a blue plaque. It opened in 1862 and closed in 1958. It was named after a chimney sweep, whose stage name was Sam Collins, and who converted a public house on the site into the music hall.

Further along Upper Street, the **parish church of St Mary**, Islington (6), is soon reached. The Abbots of Westminster had a chapel here but it is not recorded when the first church was built. During the middle ages there was a shrine dedicated to 'Our Ladie of Isledon', but this was swept away at the Reformation in the sixteenth century. Severely damaged in the Second World War, the church was rebuilt and re-dedicated in 1956; only the tower and spire remain of the eighteenth-century church designed by Launcelot Dowbiggin.

The centre of the administration of the borough of Islington is the **Town Hall** (7), designed by E. C. P. Morison and opened in 1925.

Our way leads to the **Union Chapel** (8), the leading nonconformist meeting place in the borough today. Built in 1876, to the designs of James Cubitt, it typifies the high Gothic style of the late nineteenth century.

Return from the chapel to Canonbury Lane and turn into the lane, which takes its name from the house (bury) of the Augus-

ISLINGTON

1. Site of the Angel
2. Royal Agricultural Hall
3. Statue of Sir Hugh
   Myddleton
4. Islington Green
5. Collins music hall
6. St Mary's church
7. Town Hall
8. Union Chapel
9. Canonbury Tower
10. Canonbury Place
11. Highbury Fields
12. Cross Street
13. Camden Passage
14. Duncan Terrace

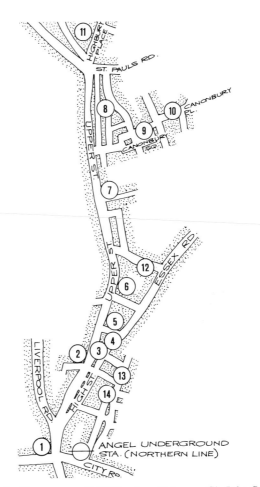

tinian Canons of St Bartholomew the Great in Smithfield, just outside the City of London. It is not far to Canonbury Square, and beyond it the remains of **Canonbury Tower** (9). The tower reminds us that in the thirteenth century Ralph de Berners gave the manor of Islington to the Canons of St Bartholomew's. The tower itself was built in the early sixteenth century during the office of William Bolton, the last prior of the order in Smithfield. His rebus, a visual pun on his name, can still be seen on a nearby house. It is an arrow (bolt) piercing a barrel (a tun), so making the word 'bolt-tun'. After the dissolution of the monastery in 1539 the property had several owners until 1570, when Alderman Sir John Spencer, who is buried in St Helen's church, Bishopsgate, bought the house and grounds for £2000. The following century the estate passed to the Compton family through marriage. Extensively restored in 1952, part of the site is now occupied by a small theatre.

Before leaving the vicinity of the tower take a walk around the square. George Orwell lived at 27B Canonbury Square in 1945. Some of the area beyond the tower has been rebuilt in recent years, while other parts have benefited from the work of conservationists (10).

Compton Road, another reminder of past lords of the manor, leads to St Paul's Road.

Turn left at the junction and you soon reach Highbury and Islington station (Victoria Line and British Rail). The road to the right of the station leads to **Highbury Fields** (11). If property developers had not taken over much of the land here, there might well have been another large park to rank with Hyde, Regent's and St James's parks. A certain Mr Lloyd tried, in vain, to raise the required sum, about £250,000, to buy the land and to turn it into a vast public park which would have been as large as Regent's Park and Hyde Park put together. Lloyd interested the Prince Consort and several members of the aristocracy in his scheme but in the end the builders won the day and left Highbury Fields only a 'poor shadow of its former glorious self' for us to enjoy in the twentieth century.

Having rested awhile in the Fields, leave by way of Baalbec Road and, following through Highbury Grove, cross St Paul's Road once more. Your route now follows St Mary's Grove, Alwyne Place and Alwyne Road to Canonbury Road. Here turn left and soon Essex Road station is reached. Turn right and soon Islington Green will come into sight once more, but first visit **Cross Street** (12) with its lovely Adam-style houses.

On reaching the Green continue past **Camden Passage** (13), where you may well be attracted to spend a little time, and probably quite a lot of money, browsing among the antique shops. Passing the Myddleton statue on your right, walk along the High Street and turn left into Duncan Street, which will lead you into **Duncan Terrace** (14), where Charles Lamb lived for a short time. His house is marked with a blue plaque.

Left: *Canonbury Tower, Islington.*
Right: *The statue of Sir Hugh Myddleton on Islington Green.*

13
Kensington

One of London's more important shopping areas, Kensington High Street offers the walker and the shopper a wide variety of choice, both in places of interest and places for shopping.

Served by both the Circle and the District Lines of the underground network, **High Street Kensington station** (1) was opened in 1868. It is surrounded by shops, some forming a pleasant arcade from the ticket office to the High Street itself.

Immediately on leaving the station turn right and pass the building now occupied by Marks and Spencer and British Home Stores. This was once the famous Derry and Toms departmental store. The **Roof garden** (2) has Spanish, Elizabethan and Dutch gardens, with waterfalls and fully grown trees. It is a private club and can be visited by appointment only.

Across the High Street is the site of the former town hall of the old borough of Kensington, built in 1878. The site is now occupied by a modern block but to the left of it still stands the former **Vestry Hall** (3), a delightful Victorian building which later served as a public library and which today is a branch of an Iranian bank.

Cross the road to Kensington Church Walk by the right-hand side of the Vestry Hall. This leads past the Alec Clifton-Taylor Memorial Garden, opened in 1991, to the **churchyard** (4) of St Mary Abbots. (Kensington Church Walk leads to a small, pretty square of shops and private residences, worth visiting.) On the south side of the churchyard is **St Mary Abbots**

church school (5) with the two eighteenth-century coloured figures depicting a boy and girl in the school uniform of the time. They are the work of Thomas Eustace and used to stand on either side of the entrance to the old school that was demolished in 1875.

Ahead is the parish church of **St Mary Abbots** (6), built in 1869-72 to the Gothic designs of Sir George Gilbert Scott (1811-78). The cloisters on the north side of the churchyard were designed by the architect's son John Oldrid Scott (1841-1913), whose Greek Orthodox cathedral stands in Moscow Road, Bayswater. The suffix to the dedication of the church refers to the area's landowner in the middle ages, the Abbey of Abingdon in Oxfordshire.

Walk between the cloisters and the church to Kensington Church Street and turn right to the parish war memorial. Across the road, projecting from the wall of a bank, can be seen the sign of **Ye Civet Cat** (7), which formerly adorned the previous building, an inn of that name.

Cross the High Street once more and walk along the shop front of Barkers. John Barker began his trading career at William Whiteley's store in Bayswater but set up his own business here in 1870. By the end of the nineteenth century he had acquired the present site, from Young Street to Derry Street. The building now houses Northcliffe Newspapers, including the *Daily Mail* and the *Evening Standard*.

To the one side of Barkers is Young Street, named after Thomas Young, a car-

The statues on the outside wall of St Mary Abbots church school, Kensington.

The door and the wall plaque at Mrs Patrick Campbell's house in Kensington Square.

penter apprentice of Sir Christopher Wren. Young later became the foreman carpenter to William III. At an elegant house on the right-hand side of Young Street lived, between 1847 and 1854, William Makepeace Thackeray (8). Here he wrote *Vanity Fair*, *Pendennis, Henry Esmond* and part of *The Newcomes.* When passing the house some time after he had left Young Street to live in Onslow Square, he said to his friend J. T. Fields, the American publisher: 'Down on your knees, you rogue, for here *Vanity Fair* was penned, and I will go down with you, for I have a high opinion of that little production myself.'

Kensington Square (9), dating from 1688, was one of the earliest squares to be built in the then suburbs of London, and it still contains some of its original houses. At **number 41** (10), on the north side of the square, lived Sir Edward Burne-Jones, the Pre-Raphaelite artist (1833-98). Charles Maurice Talleyrand-Périgord (1754-1838), better known to students of history as Talleyrand, foreign minister to Napoleon I and later ambassador to England for Louis-Philippe, lived at 37. At 40 lived Sir John Simon (1816-1904), the pioneer of public health.

On the west side of the square at **number 31** (11) lived Mrs Patrick Campbell (1865-1940) from 1900 to 1920. The talented and beautiful actress was the friend of the playwright George Bernard Shaw, in whose plays she often starred. In the south-west corner of the square is the **Convent of the Assumption** (12), with a chapel designed by George Goldie (1828-87).

Walk along the south side of the square and pass the chapel on the right-hand side. At **number 18** (13) John Stuart Mill (1806-73), the philosopher and economist, lived. It was here that, in 1848, he wrote the

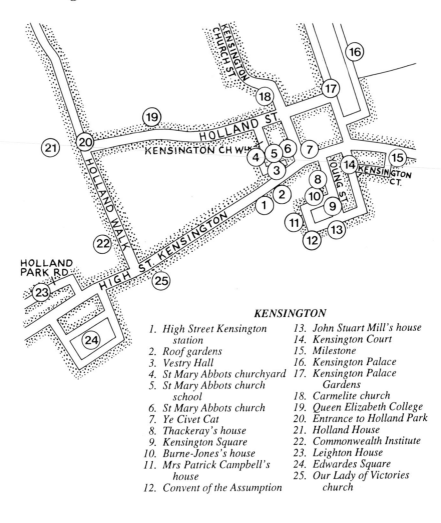

KENSINGTON

1. High Street Kensington station
2. Roof gardens
3. Vestry Hall
4. St Mary Abbots churchyard
5. St Mary Abbots church school
6. St Mary Abbots church
7. Ye Civet Cat
8. Thackeray's house
9. Kensington Square
10. Burne-Jones's house
11. Mrs Patrick Campbell's house
12. Convent of the Assumption
13. John Stuart Mill's house
14. Kensington Court
15. Milestone
16. Kensington Palace
17. Kensington Palace Gardens
18. Carmelite church
19. Queen Elizabeth College
20. Entrance to Holland Park
21. Holland House
22. Commonwealth Institute
23. Leighton House
24. Edwardes Square
25. Our Lady of Victories church

Principles of Political Economy. At the house next door, 17, lived Sir Charles Parry (1848-1918), the composer, whose best loved works include the setting to music of William Blake's 'Jerusalem'.

Leave the square by the south-east corner past numbers 11 and 12. For the Thackeray enthusiast a slight diversion at this point of the walk may be made to number 7 Kensington Square, the 'home of Lady

Castlewood' of *Henry Esmond.*

However, the route of the walk continues along Thackeray Street, where on the right-hand side is Esmond Court. At the end of the street, turn left into **Kensington Court** (14), once the largest group of Victorian mansions in London, rebuilt by Albert Grant MP in 1880. In the north-west corner of the court is a small, narrow lane that leads into Kensington High Street.

Kensington Palace.

At Kensington High Street turn right, but before crossing the road to explore Kensington Gardens look at the **milestone** (15) outside the Milestone Hotel, 1½ miles from Hyde Park Corner, one of a number of places from which distances to and from London used to be measured.

There are now 110 hectares of Kensington Gardens, whereas at the time of William III the grounds surrounding **Kensington Palace** (16) amounted to only 10 hectares. Originally the London home of the Earls of Nottingham, and called Nottingham House, it was bought by William III in 1689. Both William III and his wife died in the palace, and it remained a royal residence up to 1760, when the then Buckingham House became Buckingham Palace. At Kensington Palace the Princess Victoria was born in 1819. Outside the south front of the building stands the statue of William III, a gift from the Kaiser Wilhelm II of Germany to Edward VII.

Approach the palace through the gate into Kensington Gardens, with the boundary wall on your left. At the end of the wall turn right to visit the palace, or left, through the wall, into Kensington Palace Gardens. Here is the official entrance to the palace, most of which is taken up today with grace and favour residences, with members of the royal family having living quarters here. It was to the porch of Clock Court, on the right-hand side of the pathway, that the Archbishop of Canterbury, William Howley, went early in the morning of 20th June 1837 to tell the young Princess Victoria of her uncle William IV's death and of her accession to the throne.

Kensington Palace Gardens (17), commonly called 'Millionaires' Row', was mostly built between 1844 and 1860 and

The sunken gardens at Kensington Palace.

consists of some thirty houses, many owned by embassies. When walking away from the palace, Palace Green is on your left and facing this is number 2 Palace Green, designed by Thackeray in the Queen Anne style and lived in by him from March 1862 until his death in the following year. The plaque over the doorway is an original one designed by the Society of Arts, now the Royal Society of Arts, which initiated the commemoration of famous people on buildings associated with them. Leave by York House Place, the path by the side of Arundel House, which leads to Kensington Church Street. A short distance to the right is the Roman Catholic **Carmelite church** (18), beautifully rebuilt to the designs of Sir Giles Gilbert Scott (1880-1960), and completed shortly before his death.

After leaving the church the roadway curves around to the left. Follow it to Campden Grove, where turn left and walk along the Grove, which leads into Observatory Gardens. The noted astronomer Sir Henry South had a fully equipped observatory here from 1836 until his death in 1867. Ahead is the **Queen Elizabeth College** (19), founded originally in Kensington Square as the King's College of Household and Social Science, and renamed in 1953 in honour of Queen Elizabeth the Queen Mother, a Royal Charter being granted to the college by Queen Elizabeth II. Since 1928 it has been a school of the University of London. Follow Campden Hill Road to the junction of four roads, Campden Hill, Holland Street, Upper Phillimore Gardens and Duchess of Bedford's Walk. By walking along the last, an entrance to **Holland Park** is reached (20).

Once the private parkland of Holland House, built in the seventeenth century for Sir Walter Cope, a favourite courtier of James I, Holland Park was laid out in the West Town and the Abbot's manor. Originally called Cope's Castle, the park passed into the hands of the Holland family in the latter part of the seventeenth century, so gaining its present name. In 1952 the remaining 24 hectares of the original 80 were sold, together with the very badly bombed **Holland House** (21), to the London County Council. After restoration it was opened in 1959 by Queen Elizabeth as a memorial to her father, George VI. Today you can visit the Dutch Garden, the Japanese Garden or the former ballroom of the house, used as a refreshment pavilion. During the summer months there are open-air performances on the terrace of the house.

The entrance to the Roman Catholic church of Our Lady of Victories, Kensington.

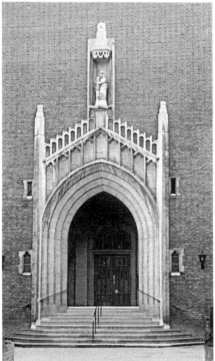

Leaving the park through the Kensington High Street gateway, one is immediately in front of the **Commonwealth Institute** (22), a fine modern building formally opened by Queen Elizabeth II in November 1962. Three floors of exhibition permanently display the history, life, scenery, natural resources and development of all the Commonwealth countries.

A short walk away in Holland Park Road is **Leighton House art gallery** (23). The house was built for Frederic, Lord Leighton (1830-96), in 1866 by George Aitchison the younger (1825-1910). The house was one of the earliest purpose-built studios in London. When Lord Leighton died his sisters offered the house and its contents to the nation, but the contents of the house were later sold. The house now displays a permanent exhibition of Victorian art, together with paintings by Leighton and his contemporaries. The studio is used for recitals, lectures and concerts.

On the south side of Kensington High Street lies **Edwardes Square** (24). According to Leigh Hunt (1784-1859), the essayist, the square was built by a Frenchman at the time of the threatened Napoleonic invasion to house 'officers and gentlemen' of the French army. So confident was the builder of the outcome of the invasion that he made his preparations well in advance of the event, which, of course, never took place. The name was taken from the family name of Lord Kensington.

Returning once more to Kensington High Street and turning right, the walker passes Earls Court Road and shortly afterwards the archway that leads into the forecourt of the Roman Catholic Church of **Our Lady of Victories** (25). Once the pro-cathedral for the Roman Catholic Diocese of Westminster, the original church was designed by George Goldie but was destroyed by bombs in the Second World War. The new church, designed by Sir Adrian Gilbert Scott, was consecrated in 1958, and is an appealing example of the simplicity of the Gothic style. From the church follow Kensington High Street back to the underground station.

Kew Palace.

14
Kew

In most people's minds Kew is synonymous with gardens and the delights of the glasshouses and hothouses of the Royal Botanical Gardens. However, the village has much more to offer than just the gardens and a short stroll in the area will reveal many places of architectural and historical interest.

Linking Kew, on the south (Surrey) side of the river, with Brentford on the north (Middlesex) side were two ferries. One was a horse ferry which was owned in the eighteenth century by Robert Tunstall, and the other, lower, ferry was known as Powel's, or the foot ferry. In February 1757 Parliament was petitioned and an Act, with royal assent, was passed in June of the same year to provide a bridge across the Thames. The site chosen was where Tunstall's ferry plied for hire, but in December 1757 Parliament was again petitioned, this time with objections to the chosen site and with recommendations that the lower ferry site should be used. In 1758 the second Act was passed and, with the petitioners' success, the bridge was duly built on the second site. Robert Tunstall financed the project, no doubt with an eye to the future revenue from the tolls. The bridge was opened by the Prince of Wales, later George III, on 4th June 1759. It lasted until 1782, when Parliament was asked to sanction its rebuilding. The second bridge, built between 1783 and 1789, had a contract price of £11,864 and James Paine (c.1716-89) as architect. Meanwhile the old wooden bridge, slightly downstream from the new one, was repaired and kept in use until Paine's bridge was finished. In 1874 the bridge was declared 'free of toll', with a compensation fee of £57,000 being paid to the owners. In 1895 steps were taken to replace the bridge once more. The Kew Bridge Act of 1898 empowered the Surrey and Middlesex County Councils to rebuild the bridge. Work began in 1899 and the present bridge was opened on 20th May 1903 by Edward VII. It was announced that it would be called 'King Edward VII's Bridge', but it is still today known as **Kew Bridge** (1).

Kew Green (2), originally an open, unfenced space of some 12 hectares, today occupies a slightly lesser area. It is certainly kept in better order now than in the eighteenth and nineteenth centuries when there were a number of complaints in the vestry minutes of rubbish being dumped on the green. Until they were abolished by the vestry in 1781, fairs were regularly held on the green, but because of the nuisance they caused the vestry acted to close them.

The parish church of **St Anne** (3) stands on the green. A private chapel at Kew in the house of Thomas and Anne Byrkis was licensed by Richard Fox, Bishop of Winchester, in 1522. This was not a parochial church or chapel but one for the private use of the Byrkis family, and there was a clause in the document reserving all rights to the vicar of Kingston, in whose parish Kew was then situated. The chapel seems to have satisfied local needs until the beginning of the eighteenth century, when in 1710 application was made for a parochial church to be built on the green. Queen Anne took an interest in the project, presented the site and gave £100 towards the building fund. Appropriately, or perhaps because of the royal patronage, the church was dedicated to St Anne, the mother of the Virgin Mary, and on 12th May 1714 was consecrated, with the vicar of Kingston preaching the sermon.

In 1851 a mausoleum was added at the east end, and later incorporated into the new (1884) chancel, for the remains of the Duke and Duchess of Cambridge. The building today is a chapel of rest for the ashes of parishioners, the Cambridge family remains having been removed to Windsor at the wish of Queen Mary, their granddaughter, whose parents, the Duke of Teck and the Duchess (née Princess Mary of Cambridge) were married in the church.

The organ, a gift to the church by George IV, is said to have been the favourite instrument of George III and also of G. F. Handel (1685-1759), both of whom played it regularly.

Tapestry pew cushions depict the history of the church. Thomas Gainsborough (1727-88), one of the founders of the Royal Academy in 1768, was buried in the churchyard near the south wall of the church. Near his grave is that of his friend Joshua Kirby (1716-74), the architect, whose works included additions to Kew church.

At the east end of the churchyard is the tomb of John Zoffany RA (1733-1810), a portrait painter of considerable reputation whose works can be seen in many galleries

The Green, Kew, with St Anne's church.

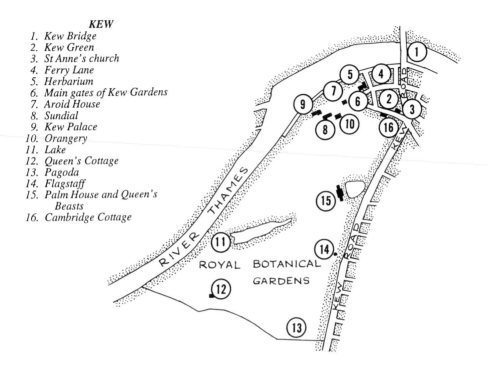

KEW
1. *Kew Bridge*
2. *Kew Green*
3. *St Anne's church*
4. *Ferry Lane*
5. *Herbarium*
6. *Main gates of Kew Gardens*
7. *Aroid House*
8. *Sundial*
9. *Kew Palace*
10. *Orangery*
11. *Lake*
12. *Queen's Cottage*
13. *Pagoda*
14. *Flagstaff*
15. *Palm House and Queen's*
    Beasts
16. *Cambridge Cottage*

ROYAL BOTANICAL GARDENS

throughout Britain.

Opposite the west door of the church is the porch of Cambridge Cottage, now a museum of the gardens (see below).

Along the north side of the green are a number of interesting eighteenth-century houses. Beside one of them runs **Ferry Lane** (4), its name reminding us of the ferries that used to ply between the Surrey and Middlesex banks of the river Thames. The short lane leads the explorer to the riverbank and, by turning left, to a pleasant walk along the riverside.

Although not open to the public, but only to *bona fide* students and qualified research workers, the **Herbarium** (5) is housed in a Georgian-style house, with later additions. It contains a splendid collection of dried plants, which forms an important depart-

ment of the Royal Botanical Gardens. There are millions of samples from all over the world, which botanists from every country come to consult. The library contains some fifty to sixty thousand volumes and is the finest taxonomic library in Europe, if not in the whole world.

At the far end of the green are the **main gates of Kew Gardens** (6). The gates and their side screens were designed by Decimus Burton (1800-81), the famous architect, whose London buildings include the Athenaeum Club (1828-30) and the arch at the top of Constitution Hill (1825-6), a memorial to the first Duke of Wellington. The gates form a fitting end to the green and a magnificent entrance to the gardens.

Kew Gardens or, to give them their correct title, the Royal Botanical Gardens, Kew,

The Orangery, Kew Gardens.

The Palm House, Kew Gardens.

The tomb of Thomas Gainsborough in the churchyard of St Anne's church, Kew.

are universally famous, cover some 110 hectares and contain as wide a variety of plants as can be seen anywhere else in the world.

Owing their origin to the private gardens of Sir Henry Capsel, who died in 1696 and who in his travels in France collected many rare trees and fruits, they have been open to the public since 1841, when Queen Victoria gave them to the nation. John Evelyn (1620-1706) makes a number of references to the gardens, commenting that there were too many trees, but admiring the glasshouses for the oranges and myrtle.

During the eighteenth century 'Capability' Brown (1715-83) landscaped the gardens and Sir William Chambers (1726-96), the architect, embellished the grounds with temples and other buildings.

Leaving the main gates, walk ahead to the first of many interesting buildings in the grounds, the **Aroid House** (7), of which the normal temperature is 27 degrees Celsius. This has an interesting history, having been initially built as part of Buckingham Palace. When John Nash (1752-1835), the Prince Regent's favourite architect, was commissioned to restore the palace, he practically rebuilt it. His design included the erection of four temple-like buildings. When

the buildings were adapted by Edward Bloner, this temple was removed and re-erected here in 1836. The house contains specimens of plants from humid tropical forests — the aroids. Because of its unusual origin the house is the oldest one of its kind in the gardens.

The seventeenth-century **sundial** (8) was erected in 1832 by William IV in the forecourt of **Kew Palace** (9). It marks the site of Kew House, which was pulled down in 1802. Kew Palace dates from 1631. Kew House and the Palace were the home of Frederick, Prince of Wales, the son of George II and father of George III. Two of the latter's sons, the Duke of Clarence (later William IV) and the Duke of Kent, father of Queen Victoria, were married here.

It is a short walk across the lawn to the **Orangery** (10). This was built in 1761, to the design of Sir William Chambers, for the Princess of Wales, whose coat of arms is carved over the central pediment of the building. The princess, Augusta of Saxe-Gotha, had married Frederick in 1737. The Orangery is one of several buildings designed for her by Chambers. Others are the Pagoda (1761-2), the Temple of Bellona (1760), the Temple of Arethusa and the Temple of Aeolus (1761). Although built to

Kew Gardens: the Aroid House.

house oranges and other exotic plants, the Orangery has over the years been used for a number of purposes, including a museum, but today houses an exhibition about Kew and the work that is done there.

To construct the artificial **lake** (11) an area of 2 hectares was excavated and a culvert, 90 metres in length, was laid to connect the former gravel pit with the river Thames. The river is the only source of water and the lake can be replenished only at high tide, and then usually only at the time of a new or full moon. Four islands of varying sizes add further to the selection of plants in the gardens by displaying, amongst others, the swamp cypress, while the banks on the Boathouse Walk side have firs. On the opposite side of the lake is Syon Vista, with its view of the river frontage of Syon House, former home of the Dukes of Northumberland, on the Middlesex bank of the river.

Although the gardens were handed over to the state in 1841 Queen Victoria retained the **Queen's Cottage** (12) until 1897. At that time she gave the cottage and the 15 hectares of woodlands surrounding it to commemorate her Diamond Jubilee. She did, however, make it a condition of the gift that they should be kept in their semi-wild state. The cottage, built in 1760 to a design by Queen Charlotte for George III and their family, was used by the royal family as a summerhouse, where picnics could be held, and later as a shooting box.

Finding one's way round Kew Gardens requires reference to the map boards, for there are some 15 miles of paths made from material excavated from the area now occupied by the lake, and the use of landmarks. One such prominent building is the **Pagoda** (13), which was erected in 1761-2 to the designs of Sir William Chambers, whose other buildings here have already been noted. Sir William's father was a Scottish merchant who was living in Stockholm at the time of his son's birth; shortly afterwards the family left Sweden and settled in Ripon, North Yorkshire. At the age of sixteen Chambers was sent to the East Indies and China with the intention of following his father's trade. He became fascinated by Chinese architecture and spent much of his time sketching. After leaving the service of the Swedish East India Company in 1749, he began his career as an architect. It was to his early youth that he turned for inspiration for the Pagoda. It stands 50 metres high with ten storeys. The building is made of stock brick and timber. The interior consists entirely of the central staircase which links the various floor levels. Although it was built in six months, its sturdiness was well put to the test in the Second World War, when a number of high-explosive bombs fell nearby.

From the Pagoda one passes next the Temperate House, a massive greenhouse designed by Decimus Burton, restored during the 1970s and reopened in 1982.

Soaring 68 metres into the sky, the **Flagstaff** (14), the fourth one to be erected in the gardens, was the gift of the people of British Columbia, presented to commemorate the centenary of the Canadian province (1958), and the bicentenary of the gardens (1959). The tree, a Douglas fir weighing 39 tons, had a diameter at the base of over 2 metres before it was shaped and was about 370 years old when it was cut down. After shaping, its weight was reduced to 15 tons and the base to 80 cm square, finally tapering to 30 cm at the tip.

Once the largest glasshouse of its kind in the world, the **Palm House** (15) was also designed by Decimus Burton; erected between 1844 and 1848, it can be compared with his similar construction at Chatsworth House, Derbyshire (1836-40), demolished in 1920, though plans and drawings of it still exist. The Palm House is just over 110 metres in length and has a crossing (transept) 30 metres wide and 20 metres high, and two wings, each of which are 15 metres wide and 9 metres high. It contains plants from the tropics of both hemispheres. The house gets its name from the wide variety of palms, or cycads, that can be seen there.

Lining the south side of the Palm House are the **Queen's Beasts**. Originally made of plaster and erected outside the specially constructed Coronation Annexe to Westminster Abbey, they were designed by James Woodford OBE, RA, and show the direct lineage of Queen Elizabeth II from Edward III (1312-77). These beasts are stone replicas of those used at the Coronation and were an anonymous gift to the gardens.

The Princess of Wales Conservatory, built during the 1980s though named after Augusta of Saxe-Gotha, houses plants of both moist and dry tropics. It is an impressive site where greenhouses full of ferns once stood.

Already mentioned as having its front entrance overlooking the green, **Cambridge Cottage** (16), dating from the eighteenth century, today houses the Wood Museum of the gardens. Once the home of the Duke and Duchess of Cambridge, it became a museum in 1910, at first being used to show British forestry. Since 1957 its function has been changed to that of a general wood and timber museum with special emphasis on timber from the Commonwealth countries. There is also a very attractive walled garden within the grounds.

15
Paddington

'A village situated on the Edgware Road, about a mile from London': this is how a writer described Paddington in 1814. It could hardly be described that way today, but there are still parts of what is now the City of Westminster that retain their village-like atmosphere. Here during Saxon times came the Paeda family, and they set up a homestead. The ending 'ton', denoting a farm or homestead, added to the family name gives us the present name of Paddington. As in other villages, life centred around the parish church of Paddington, which until the nineteenth century was St Mary's, Paddington Green, but since 1845 St James's, Sussex Gardens, has been the prime church of the 'village'.

St Mary's church, Paddington Green (1), is the third church on or near this site, the present building having been erected between 1788 and 1791 to the designs of John Plaw. Built in the form of a Greek cross, it is often taken to be a Greek Orthodox church; there was once a Greek inscription over the south doorway. It is the oldest building still standing in Paddington.

Buried in the crypt of the church, not open to the public, is Dr Barry Edward O'Meara, doctor-surgeon to Napoleon, in a grave described as being 'in the right vault under the church, right-hand avenue near the door'. However, this was all bricked over and concreted when the crypt was used as a shelter during the First World War.

The church hall, erected in classical style in 1981, features *trompe l'oeil* paintings of Sarah Siddons, Polly Perkins, John Donne, Nollekens, Hogarth and Emma Hamilton.

In the north churchyard can be seen the **grave of Sarah Siddons**, the actress (2). Her first London appearance was in 1775 at the Drury Lane Theatre, playing Portia in Shakespeare's *Merchant of Venice*, and her last performance was as Lady Macbeth at Covent Garden Theatre. Her funeral on 15th June 1831 drew over five thousand people, members of the theatre as well as of her public following.

Also in the burial ground north of the church, but in unconsecrated earth, is the **grave of Robert Haydon** (3), the artist, who in 1846 committed suicide in Burwood Place. Haydon spent the latter years of his life in Paddington painting enormous,

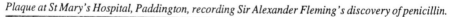

Plaque at St Mary's Hospital, Paddington, recording Sir Alexander Fleming's discovery of penicillin.

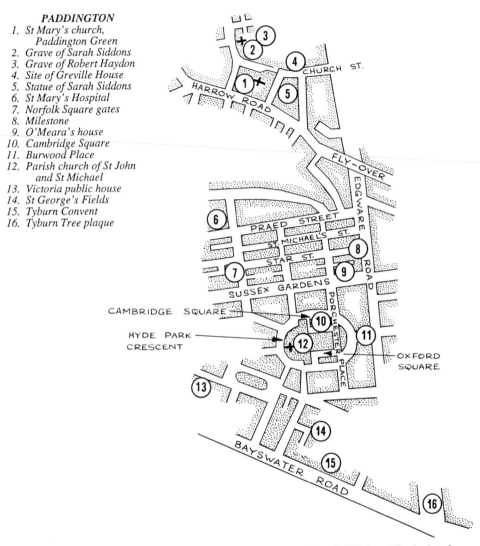

unsaleable paintings of religious and Shakespearian themes.

On the north side of Paddington Green (4), where now the Paddington Technical College stands, was **Greville House**. Here Emma Hart, or Lyon, the later Lady Hamilton (c.1765-1815), was once employed as a servant.

A **statue of Sarah Siddons** (5), depicted as the Tragic Muse and modelled on a painting by Sir Joshua Reynolds, stands on Paddington Green. It was the first statue of a woman other than a member of the royal family to be erected in London and was unveiled by Sir Henry Irving.

In a small laboratory overlooking busy

Praed Street Alexander Fleming, apparently by accident, discovered *Penicillium notatum*. By chance a mould spore blew in through an open window on to a culture dish and was dissolved by the contents of the dish. A plaque placed on the outer wall of **St Mary's Hospital** (6) records the discovery.

At the east end of **Norfolk Square** (7) there are bar-gates across the road which prevent vehicles from entering the square from Norfolk Place. In the early nineteenth century there was a reservoir here, but in 1848 All Saints church, now demolished, was built on the site, to the design of H. Clutton. The gardens have been redesigned

to make a pleasant oasis in which to relax.

On the corner of Star Street and Edgware Road, in the front window of Lloyds Bank, can be seen an ancient **milestone** (8) inscribed to the effect that Tyburn is half a mile away.

Today **number 32 Sussex Gardens** (9) is a hotel, but in the nineteenth century, when the house was number 16 Cambridge Terrace (Sussex Gardens came into being in 1938 with the renaming of Oxford and Cambridge Terraces), Barry Edward O'Meara, Napoleon's doctor, lived and died here.

To Thomas Armitage and William Ewart **Cambridge Square** (10) would be unre-

Left: *St Mary's church, Paddington Green.*
Right: *Gloucester Terrace, Paddington.*

cognisable today with all its modern buildings. But from 1866 to 1886 Thomas Armitage lived at what was then number 33, from where he strongly advocated the use of the Braille system for reading by the blind. He was the founder of the British and Foreign Blind Association, now the Royal National Institute for the Blind.

William Ewart (1798-1869) lived in the square between 1843 and his death. As a member of Parliament he was instrumental in the passing of the Act which abolished hanging in chains in 1834 and of another which in 1837 abolished capital punishment for cattle-stealing and similar offences. His attempts to get the complete abolition of capital punishment failed, although he did succeed in raising a select committee to look into the question. In 1850 he sponsored the first Public Libraries Act which brought about today's national library system by allowing local authorities to buy books from the rates for free loan to members of the public.

Burwood Place (11) is where Robert Haydon committed suicide in 1846. There is no trace today of the house in which he lived.

The **church of St John the Evangelist with St Michael and All Angels** (a church of the latter dedication was previously in Star Street but was bombed in the Second World War) in Hyde Park Crescent (12) was built in 1832 and replaced the former Connaught Chapel. It is the second oldest church in Paddington and is said to have been inspired by New College, Oxford. The architect, Charles Fowler, also built a number of market houses, including the ones at Covent Garden and Exeter.

Take Southwick Place, opposite the church, to Gloucester Square and the **Victoria public house** (13) in Strathearn Place.

Plaque at the Tyburn Convent, Paddington.

Built about 1835, it has in its Gaiety Bar upstairs all the furnishings from the former Gaiety Theatre, which once stood at the Aldwych. The downstairs restaurant, 'Our Mutual Friend', reminds us that Charles Dickens lived in the close vicinity for a few weeks in 1870 while he was working on the novel *Edwin Drood*, which he never finished.

An area that is shown on the maps of the eighteenth century as a place of execution for soldiers and which later became the burial ground for the parishioners of St George's Church, Hanover Square, today has flats built on it. Viewable from Bayswater Road, it is called **St George's Fields** (14). The burial ground was created in 1763, and it was used until it became full in 1852. Later it was used as a garden and the Royal Toxophilite Society set up its butts in a cleared portion. Laurence Sterne, author of *Tristram Shandy* and *A Sentimental Journey*, was buried here in 1768; after his burial body-snatchers removed his corpse from its grave and sold it to the professor of anatomy at Cambridge, who on seeing his late friend's body returned it immediately to London. Doubt had been sown in some people's minds as to whether or not the body had been returned to the grave, but when the area was cleared before the building of the flats all the remains of the burials were removed. Particular care was taken over the grave of Sterne and a careful examination found the body — and two heads, one of which was verified as belonging to Sterne. The complete skeleton was then reinterred in Coxwold, the tiny Yorkshire village of which he was rector.

The artist Paul Sandby, who died in 1809, was also buried here. Born in 1721 at Nottingham, he is reputed to have introduced the aquatint into England from France; certainly he and his brother Thomas used this technique. Paul produced a series of etchings of Hyde Park and a number of his prints are in the royal library at Windsor, where his brother was Deputy Ranger of Windsor Forest. In order to prevent any further body-snatching from the graveyard, two walls 2 metres high and a metre apart, were erected, in the belief that it would not be possible to throw a corpse up and over such a barrier.

Beside the **Tyburn Convent** (15) is the smallest house in London, number 10 Hyde Park Place. Only just over a metre wide, it was built to block a passage which the owner wanted to make private. The convent itself houses a Catholic religious order of nuns who, following the rule of St Benedict, dedicate their lives to the Sacred Heart by the perpetual adoration of the Blessed Sacrament. Founded in France in the nineteenth century, they were driven by the persecution of their order in 1901 from their home on Montmartre (the Mount of Martyrs) and settled here near the Hill of Martyrs — Tyburn, with its fateful gallows. In the crypt chapel there are many relics of saints who have died for their faith and at set times during the day it is possible to visit the chapel.

On a triangular road island (now inaccessible to pedestrians) opposite the Odeon Theatre, Edgware Road, is a plaque commemorating the site of **Tyburn Tree** (16). The tree, last used in 1783 for the hanging of John Austin, stood 3.5 metres high, was triangular in shape and was capable of hanging eight people on each of its three sides. It was not unusual for gallows and other places of execution to be sited at the entrance to towns as a warning to potential criminals. This tree was the place of execution for felons from Newgate Prison, as well as for the Catholic martyrs for whom the nuns perpetually pray at their convent.

The statue of the actress Sarah Siddons as the Tragic Muse on Paddington Green.

Asgill House overlooks the Thames at Richmond.

16
Richmond

The earliest mention of the town of Richmond can be found in the Anglo-Saxon Chronicle of 704, which connects the place, as does the Domesday Survey of 1086, with the manor of Kingston upon Thames, itself an ancient town, where the early Saxon kings were crowned. Sheen, as Richmond was then called, was a royal residence from the time of Henry I and was rebuilt at the time of Edward III, who died here in 1377. After the death in 1394 of Queen Anne of Bohemia her husband, Richard II, had the buildings pulled down as a token of his grief at the loss of his beloved wife and queen. A further building was destroyed by fire in 1499, so Henry VII rebuilt it once again and renamed it Richmond Palace after his Yorkshire earldom. For the Tudors the palace was a favourite retreat and it was here that Elizabeth I died in 1603. The house fell into disrepair during the Commonwealth and was ultimately demolished after the Restoration in 1660.

Richmond station (1) was rebuilt in 1937 to the designs of John R. Scott, grandson of Sir George Gilbert Scott, and is a fine example of the style of architecture developed by the former Southern Railway company between the two world wars.

Turn right on leaving the station forecourt and walk along the pavement, where an old **milestone** (2) can be seen, and find the **church of St John the Divine** (3), built between 1831 and 1836 to the designs of Lewis Vulliamy, son of Benjamin Vulliamy, the clockmaker, with a chancel added early in the twentieth century. Cross over the road, and walk back the way you have come, passing shops and public houses, and turn down one of the small roads between the shops. At the end turn left towards the Green.

Theatrical performances are not new to Richmond. Shakespeare staged performances of several of his plays at the palace for the entertainment of Elizabeth I. **Richmond Theatre** (4) was built in 1899 by Frank Matcham, whose other London theatres included the London Hippodrome in Charing Cross Road. Its interior is carefully maintained and is considered to be a fine example of the period. The first theatre at Richmond was built in the early eighteenth century and was described as a pretty barn with little porches at the front. Its successor was known as a 'Cephalic Snuff Warehouse'. Apparently patrons who bought snuff from the house would be treated to a theatrical performance at the same time. During the last few decades the theatre has continued its varied programme, which includes shows prior to transfer to the West End theatres.

Opposite the Richmond Theatre is the Little Green, given to the town by Charles II, the lord of the manor, to be used as a bowling green. **Richmond Green** (5) is one of the finest greens in the London area, and visitors to Richmond during the summer can go there to watch cricket or simply to escape from the throng of the High Street. In Tudor and Stuart times it was the centre of much activity with pageants, tournaments, joustings and other delights. Around the green there is a variety of architecture,

Richmond Theatre.

The Riverside Terrace, Richmond.

Deer in Richmond Park.

The Tudor gateway to Richmond Palace.

King's Theatre, Haymarket, paint the panels of the rooms. Another famous resident was Sir Richard Burton (1821-90), the explorer and writer, whose translation of the *Arabian Nights* is a classic of its kind.

A Tudor brick archway surmounted by the arms of Henry VII leads into the remaining portions of **Richmond Palace** (7). The Wardrobe, it is said, once housed over two thousand dresses belonging to Elizabeth I. Leave by way of the lane in the opposite corner to the archway and almost immediately ahead is **Trumpeters' Court** (8). It was known as 'The Trumpeting House' because the entrance used to be flanked by the two figures blowing trumpets which are now in the garden. The principal frontage of the house faces the river and is a good example of Georgian architecture. In the nineteenth century the house became known as the Old Palace, and Prince Metternich, the Austrian statesman, lived here in 1849 when he was forced to flee from Vienna. The house was built for Mr Hill, brother of the celebrated Abigail Hill, in 1708. Follow the pathway to Old Palace Lane, which leads down to the river Thames and to nineteenth-century cottages.

At the foot of the hill is **Asgill House** (9), built by the noted architect Sir Robert Taylor for Sir Charles Asgill, who was Lord Mayor of London in 1758. The house is built over some of the old cellars of the former royal palace, and there is a list of dates and persons associated with Richmond Palace. Cholmondley Walk along the riverside is named after the house where Lady Cowper lived in the eighteenth century, later renamed Queensberry House. It is said that Baroness Orczy had the house in mind when she wrote *The Scarlet Pimpernel*, although she had to adjust the topography of the area to suit her purposes.

notably the Cricketers public house, whose sign shows a nineteenth-century cricket match in progress on the green. There is a genial atmosphere in the Long Room Bar, while upstairs is the Lewis Room Restaurant, named after John Lewis, who in 1758 obtained permission for the reopening of Richmond Park to the public. A portrait of him hangs in the restaurant together with a tribute to him by the contemporary vicar of Richmond, the Reverend Thomas Wakefield.

Maids of Honour Row (6) was built in 1724 by command of George I to accommodate the ladies of the court who attended the Princess of Wales. In addition to living in these early grace and favour houses they each received £200 *per annum*. John James Heidegger, Master of the Revels to George I and George II, lived and died in number 4 and had the scene painters of his theatre, the

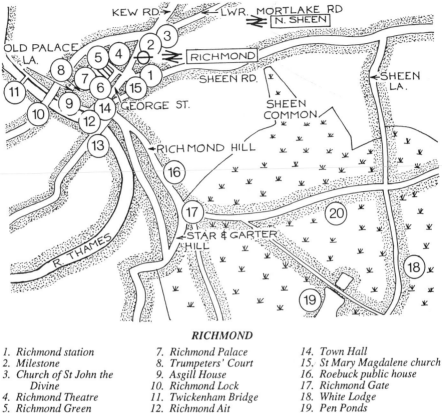

RICHMOND

1. Richmond station
2. Milestone
3. Church of St John the Divine
4. Richmond Theatre
5. Richmond Green
6. Maids of Honour Row
7. Richmond Palace
8. Trumpeters' Court
9. Asgill House
10. Richmond Lock
11. Twickenham Bridge
12. Richmond Ait
13. Richmond Bridge
14. Town Hall
15. St Mary Magdalene church
16. Roebuck public house
17. Richmond Gate
18. White Lodge
19. Pen Ponds
20. Richmond Park

To the right, at the foot of the hill from the palace, is **Richmond Lock** (10), which is built on the Surrey bank of the river and is the only lock operated by the Port of London Authority. For part of the day the weir is lifted and the river is fully tidal, but when the red disc is showing on the central arch the gates of the lock are closed. Beyond the lock can be seen **Twickenham Bridge** (11), opened in 1933 to carry the Chertsey Arterial Road. A wide concrete structure, the bridge was designed by Maxwell Ayrton.

Retrace your steps and walk along the riverside, remembering that in the spring and autumn heavy tides are liable to flood the walkway. Many a motorist has left a car along here and returned not long afterwards to find it standing in a metre of water. Islands in the river Thames are called aits or ayots, hence the **Richmond Ait** (12). Most of these islands are uninhabited and are pleasant features of the river.

Close by Richmond Bridge, on the Surrey side, is a new development of offices and residences in modern classical style, with squares and passages to explore.

Standing on the site of an ancient ferry, **Richmond Bridge** (13) was built between

1774 and 1777 to the designs of Kenton Couse, a pupil of Henry Flitcroft, the architect. The bridge was subject to tolls until 1859 and in 1937 it was widened, as can be seen by looking under the bridge and seeing the different-coloured materials. Keep to the Surrey side of the river and walk up by way of Bridge Street, noting the eighteenth-century milestone on the side of the bridge, and arrive at Hill Street. Turn left at the top of Bridge Street and shortly on the same side of the road will be found the **Town Hall** (14), built in 1893 to the designs of W. J. Ancell.

Continue on to Red Lion Street on the right and turn up it to Paradise Road. Here is Richmond parish church, dedicated to **St Mary Magdalene** (15). The main body of the church dates from 1750, with a fifteenth-century tower and twentieth-century chancel. There are a number of monuments from the previous church including a monumental brass to Robert Cotton, who died in 1591 and who was the Officer of the Wardrobe under Mary I and Elizabeth I. Major Bean, who died in 1815, has a monument designed by John Bacon Junior, while in the churchyard is the tomb of Sir Matthew Decker (1759), designed by Peter Scheemakers, whose tombs can be seen in many parish churches all over Britain as well as in Westminster Abbey.

To reach Richmond Park it is necessary to retrace one's steps back to Richmond Bridge and to continue to walk beyond the end of Bridge Street. At the fork in the road take the left-hand road and find the **Roebuck public house** (16), built in the eighteenth century. Continue past the Star and Garter House by E. M. Barry, third architect son of Sir Charles Barry, and enter the park by way

of **Richmond Gate** (17).

Ahead of you stretch 1000 hectares of parkland, containing herds of both red and fallow deer and the Isabella Plantation with magnificent displays of rhododendrons, heathers, primulas and water plants growing near the stream that runs through the trees. It is hard to believe when wandering through the parkland that London is only a few minutes away by train. The park was first created by Charles I, who enclosed the area as a hunting preserve; it is recorded that on 28th August 1647 he killed a stag and a buck in the park. Throughout the seventeenth and eighteenth centuries the park was a popular hunting place. The **White Lodge** (18) was built by Roger Morris between 1727 and 1729 and was a favourite hunting lodge of George II and his wife, Queen Caroline of Anspach. The Duke and Duchess of York, later George VI and Queen Elizabeth, lived here after their marriage. Today the lodge is the home of the Royal Ballet School.

Although there are over two dozen ponds in the park the ones that attract the most attention are probably the **Pen Ponds** (19), roughly in the middle of the park. Fish abound in the ponds and as many as ten different kinds have been found. During the Second World War the ponds were drained to prevent their use as landmarks by hostile aircraft.

Richmond Park (20) offers so much to the visitor that a pleasant hour or two can be enjoyed by simply walking around the paths that cross the grassland. But beware of the deer: while they can be very friendly, at other times they may be dangerous.

17
Stoke Newington

The interpretation of the name Stoke Newington reveals that it dates from Saxon times and means a new town (*ton*) in or near to a wood. With the setting up of the new London boroughs in the 1960s Stoke Newington became part of the London Borough of Hackney, from which it had been separated since the end of the nineteenth century.

In medieval times social life centred round the parish church and manor house. Ermine Street, the Roman road that runs along the boundary, brought visitors passing through on their travels to or from the City of London. By the sixteenth century Stoke Newington had acquired some importance, but little remains of this period. However, some large houses of the seventeenth and eighteenth centuries can still be seen.

Built on the site of a row of Georgian houses, the 'new' **Town Hall** of Stoke Newington (1) was opened in 1937. Although no longer the centre of local government, it still serves the local community in other ways. From its forecourt can be seen the two parish churches of the village.

Next to the Town Hall, with the Reference Library built on to it, is the **Central Lending Library** (2), erected in 1892, only two years after the Vestry adopted the Public Libraries Act. In the entrance hall is the memorial to local men killed in the First World War and there is an exhibition hall used for local prints and a collection of paintings. On permanent display in the hall is a fine bust of Daniel Defoe, who lived in the parish during the early eighteenth cen-

tury. There is also a commemorative plaque to Edgar Allan Poe, who attended the Manor House School.

The corner of Church Street and Edwards Lane was the site of the **Manor House School**, and Poe's association with it is marked by a blue plaque (3). Poe stayed in England between 1815 and 1820. His headmaster, Dr Dransby, was also the pastor of the local church and Poe describes his ascent into the pulpit on a Sunday morning in *William Wilson*. The headmaster said that Poe, 'who went under the name of Allan', was 'likable', but 'his parents spoilt him by allowing him too much pocket money. He was intelligent, wayward and wilful.'

Church Street (4) contains an interesting selection of domestic architecture from the seventeenth to twentieth centuries. The elegant houses that face the end of Edwards Lane are typical of the early seventeenth century: red brick, white sash windows, a doorway to the hall and the front room of the ground floor in which to receive guests, with a simple ironwork railing.

A house on the corner of Defoe Road is marked with a blue plaque recording that **Daniel Defoe** lived here (5). The actual house in which he lived was demolished in 1865, when the present one was built, and is described as being 'gloomy and of irregular bricks'. Here Defoe wrote his most famous book, *Robinson Crusoe*, which was first published in 1719, two years after he moved to Stoke Newington. He also wrote here one of his pamphlets that led to his being fined, pilloried and imprisoned: *The Short-*

est *Way with Dissenters;* later came *Moll Flanders* and *A Journal of the Plague Year.*

Shortly after leaving the site of Defoe's house, on the same side of the road, there is a short **terrace of houses** dating from the late seventeenth or early eighteenth century (6). Notice in particular the decorated overmantels of the doorways. Nearby, set back from the present pavement, is another pair of houses from the eighteenth century.

On the opposite side of the road, the only reminders of the former house and grounds of **Abney Park** (7) are the entrance gateway and wrought-iron railings. Built at the end of the seventeenth century, the house was later used as a training college for Wesleyans. A large area of the grounds was turned into the Abney Park Cemetery in the nineteenth century.

The name of **Fleetwood Street** (8) commemorates the large and handsome house that once stood here, occupied by a distinguished Cromwellian soldier, Colonel Fleetwood. At the Restoration of the Monarchy in 1660 he was fortunate in receiving no punishment other than being 'perpetu-

(Above) memorial to Isaac Watts and (right) the grave of General Booth and his wife at Abney Park Cemetery, Stoke Newington.

STOKE NEWINGTON
1. Town Hall
2. Central Lending Library
3. Site of Manor House
   School
4. Seventeenth-century houses
5. Site of Daniel Defoe's
   house
6. Houses of c.1700
7. Abney Park
8. Fleetwood Street
9. Site of John Wilmer's house
10. Three Crowns public house
11. Number 187 Stoke
    Newington High Street
12. Abney Park Cemetery
    entrance
13. Presbyterian church
14. New River
15. Clissold Park
16. Parish church of St Mary
17. New St Mary's church
18. Newington Green

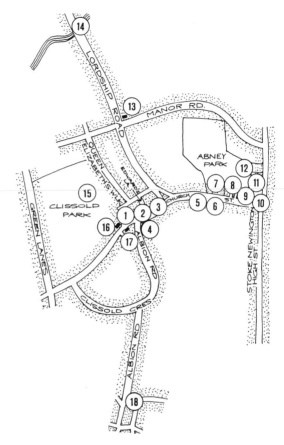

ally incapacitated from all offices of trust', even though he had married Bridget, the widow of General Ireton and daughter of Oliver Cromwell. The house was demolished in 1872 and the materials were used to build the houses on the site of its gardens. Parts of the finely carved ceiling are preserved at the public library.

One of the most unusual burials of all time took place in Stoke Newington in 1764: a local Quaker by the name of John Wilmer lived in fear of being buried alive and left specific instructions in his will that he should be buried in a bed with a table and chair by the side of it in case he awoke from his 'sleep'. In addition a wire was to be attached to his wrist and connected to a bell in the coachman's house. But the family waited in vain for the summons. The wire rusted and was cut off from the bell, and the garden was built over, although many say that he still lies there on his bed waiting to wake up. Part of the **site of John Wilmer's house** and garden is now occupied by a timber yard (9).

Shortly after the timber yard Church Street joins Stoke Newington High Street and on the corner stands the **Three Crowns public house** (10). It was so named after the three crowns of England, Scotland and Ireland to

The ornate Georgian doorway of a house in Church Street, Stoke Newington.

mark the progress through the area of James I of England (James VI of Scotland) when he came to claim the throne of England on the death of Elizabeth I in 1603.

Leaving the Three Crowns tavern, turn left. On the same side of the road are two interesting eighteenth-century houses. **Number 187** (11) is shown on earlier maps as Halfway House. It is now used as council offices. Its neighbour is also in use as offices, but number 191 no longer serves its former purpose as a hostel for fallen women.

The entrance to **Abney Park Cemetery** (12) looks like the forecourt of an Egyptian temple. But the cemetery, in the grounds of the former Abney Park House, has suffered from neglect over the past few years. However, it is well worth making a short exploration of it. Here are buried General Booth, the founder of the Salvation Army,

and his wife, while under the church Bridget Fleetwood, Oliver Cromwell's daughter, was buried. There is also a life-size memorial by the sculptor E. H. Bailey to Isaac Watts, who lived at one time in Fleetwood House, although he is actually buried in Bunhill Fields in central London. The architect of the cemetery, opened in 1840, was William Hoskings, later Professor of Architecture and Engineering Construction at King's College, London.

Returning to the entrance of the cemetery, turn left and walk up towards Stamford Hill. When Manor Road is reached turn left once again and walk along to the **Presbyterian church** (13), on the corner of Lordship Road. Turn right up Lordship Road and about a quarter of a mile along there is a tiny bridge over some water. This is the **New River** (14), engineered in the early seventeenth century by Hugh Myddleton, bringing fresh water from Ware in Hertfordshire to Stoke Newington. Originally the open channels continued to Rosebery Avenue, near Sadlers Wells Theatre. Today the water is fed into the huge reservoirs here and, after filtering in the nearby Green Lanes waterworks pumping station, is piped to the taps of the metropolis. The old pumping house seen on the skyline dates from 1854. It was designed by Chadwell Mylne to look like a medieval castle because the local inhabitants had objected to the erection of the pumping station on the grounds that it would spoil the view from their houses.

Retrace your steps to Manor Road. Then turn right along Lordship Park until Queen Elizabeth's Walk is reached. Turn left along the Walk to **Clissold Park** (15), which covers 22 hectares. It takes its name from the Reverend Augustus Clissold, who was curate at the parish church. He married one of the daughters of Mrs Crawshay, the owner of the house and grounds, and so came into possession of them. Later the property was put up for sale and two local residents, John Runtz and Joseph Beck, brought about its purchase as a public park for £96,000. The two benefactors are commemorated on a granite fountain in the centre of the park. The former residence, built in 1790, is now used as a refreshment place. Tennis courts, a children's playground, a bowling green and a bandstand are other facilities. The lakes here, once claypits, dug to make bricks for the house, are now the home of waterfowl. The New River also flows through part of the park and in the winter gulls swoop over the heads of strollers.

When Stoke Newington was a small village the spiritual needs of the parish were well cared for by the small **parish church of St Mary** (16). Originally medieval, the present church was 'newly re-built' in 1563 by the lord of the manor, William Patten, whose coat of arms is over the south-east doorway. Inside there is a memorial to John Dudley, whose widow, Elizabeth, married Thomas Sutton, the founder of the Charterhouse in the City.

Across the road from St Mary's, a new church designed by Sir George Gilbert Scott was consecrated in 1858; the spire was added later by his son, John Oldrid Scott.

Left: *The old parish church of St Mary, Stoke Newington.*

Right: *New St Mary's church, Stoke Newington, was designed by Sir George Gilbert Scott.*

The church is a noble building without and within, and it has been suggested that should the Diocese of London ever be split up this church could become the cathedral of North London. **New St Mary's church** (17) has a number of interesting memorials, including one to the Reverend Thomas Jackson, vicar of the parish from 1852 to 1886, during which time the transfer from the old to the new church took place. Both churches were bombed in the Second World War, and the congregation worshipped in the old church until the new one was completely restored in the 1950s.

Now walk from the Town Hall down Albion Road to **Newington Green** (18); although not strictly in the parish of Stoke Newington, it is a rewarding place at which

to finish. The Unitarian Chapel was built in 1708, when this area was being settled by nonconformists, who had been ejected from the Church of England under the Act of Uniformity of 1662. In addition to chapels, academies of education for their ministers and lay preachers were firmly established here. Mary Wollstonecraft rented a house on the Green and opened a school for twenty pupils; her pamphlets on education and the rights of women brought her into contact with some of the leading thinkers of her time. She married William Godwin and their daughter, Mary, who married Shelley the poet, wrote the novel *Frankenstein*. As late as 1859 the Green is described as being of a rural nature; today the Green remains but rural England has moved away.

Index